Ainsworth Rand Spofford

A Practical Manual of Parliamentary Rules

Ainsworth Rand Spofford

A Practical Manual of Parliamentary Rules

ISBN/EAN: 9783337155377

Printed in Europe, USA, Canada, Australia, Japan

Cover: Foto ©Suzi / pixelio.de

More available books at **www.hansebooks.com**

A

PRACTICAL MANUAL

OF

PARLIAMENTARY RULES,

COMPILED FOR THE READY REFERENCE OF

SOCIETIES, CONVENTIONS, PUBLIC MEET-
INGS, AND DELIBERATIVE AND
LEGISLATIVE ASSEMBLIES.

BY

AINSWORTH R. SPOFFORD,

Librarian of Congress.

Editor of "The American Almanac and Treasury of Facts,"
"The Library of Choice Literature," etc.

A. H. ANDREWS & CO., PUBLISHERS.
CHICAGO, ILL.
1884.

TABLE OF CONTENTS.

———•———

Introduction.

RULES for organization, and for the conduct of business, stand at the foundation of all progress in legislation. Equally essential are they to the harmonious and successful transaction of the business of public meetings or voluntary assemblies of all kinds. In this country the forum of debate is so wide, and the personal freedom of the citizen so absolute, that there is peculiar necessity for some standard of common appeal, which shail forward the objects of every assembly, without undue restriction of its individual members. An unorganized assembly is a mob, and a mob without a leader. The object of all parliamentary rules is, or should be, to organize the will of the assembly into orderly action. While every parliamentary body has its parties, and almost every deliberative assembly develops marked differences of opinion, a firm adherence to just rules, administered by an impartial presiding officer, will commonly insure the prevalence of the will of the majority, which, under free government, is assumed to be the supreme law.

It is the aim of this brief Manual to combine, in a succinct and business-like order, those principles of parliamentary law most generally recognized by the latest authorities on this subject. Many extensive treatises exist, some of which, though valuable, are so antiquated as to be unsafe guides. Many special Manuals contain,

7

with great fullness, the rules and precedents governing special legislative bodies. While all these have been drawn upon, and the variations in practice between the law of the British Parliament and the rules now in force in the Congress of the United States are often stated, it has been the aim of the compiler to make a book of practical utility in the conduct of business in voluntary societies and public meetings. While organized associations exist in the United States to the number of many thousands, in all of which a knowledge of what may be called well-established parliamentary rules is important, it is absolutely essential in State conventions (*e. g.* to frame a constitution), political conventions, ecclesiastical bodies (as the Presbyterian General Assembly, or the General Convention of the Protestant Episcopal Church), municipal councils, many incorporated associations, and in public meetings of a deliberative character. In all these it is of cardinal importance that the time of the assembly, always limited, should not be consumed by frivolous matters, ignorant pretenders to knowledge, or rambling debate, to the obstruction of the business which is the main object of meeting. To arrive at a clear expression of the will of the majority, and to arrive at it in the shortest time compatible with a fair hearing for opposing views, should be the object alike of the rules and of the officers appointed to administer them. Any other theory, which should give individual license free play in a deliberative assembly, would be destructive of the very objects of its organization, and would subordinate the rights of the majority to the whims or caprice of a factious minority.

CHAPTER I

Membership.

THE first element important to be determined in any organized assembly, whether legislative or deliberative, is, who are entitled to participate in its proceedings. This question, as regards the constitution of legislative bodies, is always fixed by law or constitution—the members having regular credentials being placed upon a roll of members, and sworn in as legislators. Disputed elections or contested seats are considered at a later period, although cases have arisen in Congress (notably the New Jersey contested election, in 1839,) in which the House of Representatives remained unorganized for days, by a struggle between parties as to which set of claimants should be admitted to Congress. In conventions, and other representative bodies of a permanent though not legislative character, the qualifications of delegates or members are commonly defined by the constitution or by-laws of the body. In less

9

permanent representative bodies, or in conventions specially called, the assembly itself decides who shall be admitted to seats, unhampered by the rules of former conventions of the same kind. Where those presenting themselves as members bring credentials of any kind, the holders are either admitted to their seats unquestioned, or doubtful or conflicting credentials are referred to a Committee on Credentials, when appointed, whose report is commonly accepted as final by the full assembly. In some cases, rival claimants to seats are both admitted, with or without the right to vote; and, sometimes, in political conventions, contesting delegations are granted half a vote to each member, for the sake of party harmony, and to avoid consuming time over bitter factional feuds.

In more informal public gatherings and voluntary assemblies, whose members bring no credentials, the right to take part in the proceedings is assumed to belong to all present. There is no roll of members, and many of the rules which would be imperative in an organized deliberative body, it would here be impossible to enforce.

The qualifications for membership in Congress require that a Senator shall be thirty years of age, nine years a citizen of the United States, and a resident of the State wherein he was chosen. In the case of a Representative, he must be twenty-five years of age, seven years a citizen of the United States, and an inhabitant of the State in which he has been elected. The Clerk of the House preceding the one about to organize must, by law, make up a roll of members, placing on it those only whose credentials are regular. The legal disqualifications for membership are: interest in government contracts, holding another office, being a Presidential elector, or practicing in the Court of Claims.

In Great Britain, any subject is qualified for election to the House of Commons who is twenty-one years of age, except peers, clergymen of the Church of England, contractors, bankrupts, and certain officials. Members of the French *Corps Législatif* are admitted to seats on a *prima facie* claim, the validity of their election being afterwards examined by committees.

CHAPTER II.

Organization.

THE first step in the organization of any assembly is for some one to call the body to order. In the Senate this is the duty of the Vice-President or of the President *pro tempore*. In the House of Representatives it is the duty of the Clerk of the preceding House to call the members to order pending the roll-call, 'the election of a Speaker as permanent presiding officer, and the swearing-in of the members elect. In ecclesiastical and some other conventions, the Moderator of the preceding convention, or the Clerk, calls to order. In national political conventions, this duty devolves upon the Chairman of the Executive Committee of the party. In less formal assemblies, and in all voluntary meetings, any person present may make the call. It is usual (though by no means universal) to elect a temporary Chairman in public assemblies of a deliberative character. This may be done on the motion of

12

the person calling the assembly to order, or at his suggestion by another member, in either case the assembly signifying assent by voting aye; or, the one calling the meeting to order may simply request another by name to take the chair. In this case, however, courtesy to the assembly demands that the request should be put hypothetically—" if there be no objection." The motion for a temporary Chairman may be put either with or without a second. The nays, however, should be called for, and the motion should not be announced as prevailing unless it has received a manifest majority of voices. If adopted, the person selected is to take the chair at once. It is usual at this stage for the temporary Chairman (with or without a speech of thanks) to call for the nomination of a Secretary *pro tem*. This motion, made by any one, and duly seconded, is put to vote and customarily adopted. This completes the temporary organization of the assembly. At this stage, or later, it is sometimes moved and carried that the rules for the government of the body be those governing the House of Representatives, wherever applicable, or a Committee on Rules may be appointed on motion of any member that such committee be nominated by the Chair. This committee, after consultation, may bring in a code of rules (the fewer and simpler the better) to govern the debates and proceedings of the body; or they may recommend the adoption of the rules of the House of Representatives, or of some Manual of parliamentary law. In any case, adherence to some systematic rules, with a firm and impartial application of them by the Chair, and a cheerful acquiescence in them by the assembly, is essential to good order, to harmony, and to the successful accomplishment of the business in hand.

At this stage in the proceedings, or earlier, the Chair may state the object of the meeting, or may call upon some member to do it. The only actual business which can properly be transacted before a permanent organization would seem to be this statement of the object of the meeting, reading the call for its assembling, if any, or providing for the enrollment of a list of members to be taken by the Secretary, if deemed desirable. The next step, commonly, is for the Chair to appoint a Committee on Permanent Organization, usually upon the motion of one member, seconded by another. Where, however, the members are a constituent body, the appointment of a Committee on Credentials is a part of the preliminary business, before proceeding to permanent organization. This committee should be appointed by the Chair on the motion of any one present, duly seconded and put to vote.

In many, and indeed in most cases, it is usual for the assembly to dispense wholly with the double form of temporary and permanent organization, or else to adopt a motion that the temporary officers elected be continued as the permanent officers of the assembly. In all voluntary assemblies, having no permanent rules to control their action, this is the simpler and the time-saving method of organization. In more formal bodies, the Committee on Permanent Officers should make a report with as little delay as possible, in order not to keep business waiting, no general business being in order until the assembly is permanently organized. The permanent officers being reported

by name from the chairman of the committee
on that subject, the President *pro tem.* at once
puts the questions *seriatim* to the assembly,
which usually ratifies, by a *viva voce* vote, the
selection of the committee. To the President
and Secretary is sometimes added an officer
designated as Sergeant-at-Arms or Doorkeeper,
to preserve order, with power to appoint assistants. In still other cases, a number of Vice-
Presidents are nominated and chosen—an hon-
orary custom intended to give weight to the
meeting by their names—and these gentlemen
usually take seats on the platform. It is sometimes the case that the election of permanent
officers is required to be by ballot, when several
candidates may be voted for, for each office;
but this, in the case of meetings convened for
a temporary purpose, is very seldom proposed,
as it may consume much time. In fact, in this
matter, as in all others concerning the proceedings, time is of supreme importance to men
with whom the prompt dispatch of business
has become a rule of life.

The permanent organization of legislative
bodies is fixed by law or constitution, or both.

In the House of Representatives, a Speaker
must be elected *viva voce* directly after the
Clerk has completed the roll-call of members
elect. Two or more candidates for the office
of Speaker are usually nominated by their party
friends. To elect a Speaker a majority of the
votes cast is required, although this rule was
suspended in the case of the protracted dead-
lock between the Republicans and Democrats
in the session of 1855–56, the American party
holding the balance of power, so that no
one of three candidates could be elected. The
House continued unorganized for nine weeks,
until it agreed to a resolution that a plurality of
votes should elect, and N. P. Banks was chosen
Speaker. The same delay in organizing the
House occurred in the Thirty-sixth Congress,
1859–60, when a dead-lock of two months was
broken on Feb. 1, 1860, by the election of Mr.
Pennington as Speaker, though the majority
rule was not suspended. Upon the election of
a Speaker, the Clerk declares the result, and the
Speaker-elect is conducted to the chair by two
of the members who were rival candidates for
the office. The oath of office is then adminis-

tered to him by that member who has served longest continuously in the House. After calling the House to order, the next business is the qualification of all the members by taking the oath to support the Constitution. This is administered by the Speaker, reading it from the book to bodies of members presenting themselves in convenient numbers in front of the Speaker's desk. Next after the election of Speaker, the House chooses a Clerk by *viva voce* vote; also a Sergeant-at-Arms, Doorkeeper, Postmaster, and Chaplain. In the Senate of the United States, which, unlike the House, is a continuous body, not requiring a new organization, as to officers, every two years, the Vice-President calls the Senate to order, either on the 4th of March (if called in special session by the President), or the first Monday in December. New Senators, or others who have been re-elected, are then sworn in, and the Secretary and other officers are either continued or their successors are elected, at any time, according to the will of the majority.

The organization of the British Parliament is attended with great formality. The Lords, being a permanent body, announce to the House of Commons that they are ready to receive them, and request, through the Lord Chancellor, that they will choose their Speaker. The day after, the Speaker-elect appears at the bar of the House of Lords, at the head of the Commons (or as many of them as may attend), and makes formal claim of " all their ancient and undoubted rights and privileges." This is followed by the Queen's speech, the taking of the oath by all the members, and the adoption of an address in answer to the royal speech. Before these ceremonies, Parliament can proceed with no business.

CHAPTER III

Sessions.

THE term Session may denote: first, the time occupied by the sitting of any assembly after organizing for the day, until the adjournment; or, secondly, the time spent in public business by a legislative assembly, from the first meeting of the members, until their adjournment to the next session. This time is usually several months. The first-named use of the term Session is synonymous with "meeting," or with "sitting." In societies, meetings are usually held at fixed intervals, defined in the rules or by resolution. These meetings are ordinarily closed by a simple motion of adjournment. This may be either "without day," or without qualification of any kind, and in either case this ends the session definitively, the assembly not meeting again; or, if a permanently organized body, convening at the time fixed by their rules for the next regular meeting. Or, in the third place, adjournment may be to a future time specified. When an assembly meets several days consecutively, and adjourns, having completed the objects of convening it, the meetings all constitute one session, although embracing several sittings. Instead of a regular adjournment, a recess is often taken by an assembly, this term being equivalent to an intermission.

Some societies have fixed hours both for beginning and closing their meetings. This is business-like, and conducive to efficient condensation of speech and action on the part of the members.

In Congress, the daily sessions of Senate and House have been for many years begun at 12 M., except during the later stages of an annual session, when one or both Houses may resolve to meet at 11 A. M., or in some cases still earlier. As most of the committee work is done during the forenoon hours, this secures a fuller attendance in the House. The length of the daily sittings varies greatly, from a few minutes each day in the early part of the session, before committee business is prepared, to many hours in the busier season, often extending (with an interval of recess for dinner, at 5 or 6 P. M.) far into the night.

The legislative day begins on the meeting of the House or Senate, and terminates with the adjournment, but does not always coincide with the day as marked by the calendar. Thus, the legislative day which concludes the session of Congress in the alternate years is styled March 3d in the journals and *Record*, although it is actually March 4, from the hour of midnight, to 12 M. of this day which terminates the existence of a Congress. Although its sittings are almost invariably confined to week-days, Congress does not necessarily adjourn at the beginning of Sunday; a majority may continue in session after that hour (as has frequently happened in the pressure of business), but the journal bears the date of the day preceding— Saturday.

In the British Parliament no less than four Sunday meetings of that body, occasioned by the demise of the sovereign, have occurred, and on several occasions of great political interest or excitement, the debate in the Lords or the Commons has been prolonged into Sunday morning.

An annual session of Congress is required by the Constitution, although that body may meet more frequently, either on its own motion (by adjourning to meet on a day fixed), or when summoned in special session by the President. The beginning of the session is constitutionally fixed as the first Monday in December, unless Congress by law appoints a different day. The annual session must terminate on the 4th of March, at noon, in every alternate year—*i. e.*, the odd years, 1885, 1887, etc.—when the term of a Congress expires. In the even years, when this limitation does not exist, the session continues from five to nine months. There are great disadvantages connected with these irregular annual sessions of Congress. Conspicuous among these is the fact that there is an interregnum of nine months occurring each alternate year, extending from March 4 to the first Monday in December, during which Congress is unorganized, and without power to organize by its own motion. Secondly, there is no Speaker of the House of Representatives for the same long period, while, by existing law, this officer may be required to assume the office of President of the United States in a certain event. Thirdly, the entire legislative business of the nation is necessarily crowded every other year into about sixty days (exclusive of the holiday vacation, Sundays, etc.), with most pernicious results to the character of the legislation. Fourthly (and, perhaps, most important) the members of the House of Representatives, elected as they are under this system more than one year before they can take their seats in Congress, do not represent the popular will as if freshly sent from the people. The suggestion has been made that all these difficulties might be removed, and adequate and proper time for legislation secured every year by newly-elected Representatives, were each Congress required to be organized (as are nearly all of the State Legislatures) early in January following the November in which its members were elected. The political year might begin, like the calendar year, January 1, and Congress would find adequate time for maturing its legislation, instead of being subject to the hasty and half-considered methods which now sometimes prevail.

Congress may be constitutionally convened at any time when not in session, "on extraordinary occasions, by proclamation of the President"—a power which has been exercised no less than twelve times since the beginning of the government in 1789. These special sessions have been called : (1) after the death of the President ; (2) on occasions of commercial distress which appeared to demand fiscal legislation ; (3) to meet emergencies in time of war, as in the war of 1812–15, and the civil war of 1861 ; (4) to enact necessary appropriation laws which had been lost by disagreement between the two Houses in the Congress just expired.

The President is also clothed by the Constitution with the power to adjourn both Houses of Congress to such time as he shall think proper, in case of disagreement between them as to the time of adjournment (Art. 2, Sec. 3), but this prerogative has never yet been exercised.

In the British Parliament, which, like Congress, must meet annually, the sessions customarily last from February to August. Short special sessions are also held when public

emergency demands. The daily sessions customarily begin at 4 o'clock P. M. and frequently continue far into the night.

Secret Sessions.

In all parliamentary bodies the power to
order that certain meetings for the consideration of executive business shall be secret, is
regarded as the privilege of the body. This is,
of course, subject to any provision in the law or
constitution governing the body that all ses- .
sions shall be open, as is the universal rule regulating courts of justice. In the United States
Senate, sessions for the consideration of executive business are held with closed doors. Executive business includes the consideration, with
a view to confirmation or rejection, of nominations to office made by the President, and the
ratification or rejection of proposed treaties
with foreign powers. It may also include the
consideration of any measure, the discussion of
which it is not deemed prudent, for reasons of
State, to make public. The latest instance of
such secret sessions was when the Senate debated, in 1884, the proposed amendment to

the consular and diplomatic appropriation bill, placing the sum of $250,000 at the disposal of the Executive to negotiate the purchase of an isthmus canal-franchise through Nicaragua. An executive session may be moved by any Senator at any stage of the open or legislative session, though they are more frequently held near the close of the day. If the motion that the Senate proceed to the consideration of executive business has a majority, the Senate chamber is cleared of all persons except certain clerks and assistants sworn to secrecy. The Senate rules require that all remarks, votes and proceedings in executive session shall be kept secret until the Senate shall, by resolution, take off the injunction of secrecy. Any Senator disclosing such secret proceedings is liable to expulsion from the body, and any officer of the Senate divulging these secrets is liable to dismissal and to punishment for contempt. Notwithstanding these stringent provisions of the rules, custom appears to have established the prompt publication (often, doubtless, inaccurate in details) of the votes and even the purport of the speeches in secret sessions of the Senate. Nominations

to office in executive session are first referred
to committees. It requires unanimous consent
to confirm any nomination on the day it is received or reported from a committee. No ex-
tract from the executive journal can be given out
without a special order of the Senate. A majority of Senators present is sufficient to confirm
any nomination. The ratification of a treaty
requires the concurrence of two-thirds of the
Senators present; so also does a motion to
postpone a treaty indefinitely; but all other
questions, amendments, etc., upon a treaty are
decided by a majority vote.

Up to the second session of the Third Congress (November, 1794,) all the sessions of the
Senate, legislative as well as executive, were held
with closed doors. At that time the Senate
ordered that the legislative session should be
open to the public, a rule ever since maintained, although it is in the power of a majority of the Senate, at any time, to order it otherwise.

The 30th rule of the House of Representatives also authorizes secret sessions to receive
confidential communications from the Presi-

dent, or whenever the Speaker or any member shall inform the House that he has communications which he believes ought to be kept secret for the present; and by the 2d rule, the elective officers of that body must be sworn to keep the secrets of the House. But no session of the House of Representatives has, in fact, been made secret for many years. Instances of such sessions occurred during the war of 1812–15 with Great Britain, and during the Mexican war.

In the British Parliament the presumption of law is that none but the members can be present, yet there are always a limited number of spectators in each House, unless (as seldom happens) a member moves, and the House orders, the exclusion of strangers during some discussion which it is deemed expedient to keep secret. Orders are sometimes made for the withdrawal of strangers, but this does not extend to the ladies' gallery, which is not supposed to be within the House.

Joint Sessions.

Both Houses of Congress are required by the Constitution to meet together when the votes for President and Vice-President are counted. This may or may not be a joint convention, and may be held in the hall of the House of Representatives or elsewhere, as the two Houses may determine by rule or resolution. There is no instance of a meeting of the Senate and House in one body, except for this purpose, and for occasional funeral or other ceremonials where no business is done.

CHAPTER IV

Order of Business.

AFTER the permanent organization of any assembly is effected, the most important question immediately arising, is the order of procedure. In the case of a convention, a committee usually reports an Order of Business, which is adhered to, unless the assembly otherwise determine. In a society, or continuing body, the first business in order usually is the reading of the minutes of the last meeting, by the Secretary. The Chair then calls for any suggested corrections or amendments to the minutes, or announces, in the absence of such motion, that they will be considered as approved. The next business of a society or assembly holding stated meetings usually is, to receive the reports of any committees, whether standing or special (the former being first in order), or of the Secretary or other officer or board of officers to whom has been committed the transaction of any business, or the consideration of any subject which may require report to the whole body. It is usual to move that a report be accepted, and this preliminary motion is one of courtesy, bringing it formally before the body, but not equivalent to adopting or approving it finally. On the contrary, such reports are open to discussion, the Chair usually saying : "Are there any remarks upon this report?" Sometimes the debate leads to amendments being offered to some details of the report, or to the proposing of a substitute changing its entire tenor. The Chair takes the question upon the motion that the report be adopted (or amended, as the case may be, this being first in order), and announces the decision of the body according to the majority vote. Sometimes a report may be recommitted, with instructions to alter its tenor.

After the disposition of any reports, it is usual to take up the unfinished business or matters postponed from a previous session; and after that, any new business may be brought before the assembly, either by the Chair (who may have communications, memorials, etc., to present), or by the motion of any member.

In all well-organized assemblies, no one can address the Chair or take up the time of the members, unless there be a formal motion before the body. If speeches are attempted in this irregular manner, it is the duty of the Chair to inform the speaker that there is no question before the assembly, and that he is out of order. He must then take his seat, unless he has a motion to present. It sometimes happens in large assemblies, which are apt to be rather tumultuous bodies, that one or more vociferous members will insist on being heard out of order, and the only course to be pursued by a competent presiding officer is to insist upon and enforce the strict parliamentary rule that all business and debate shall be proceeded with in order. If this is done firmly and good-humoredly on the first occasion of interruption to orderly proceeding, the Chair will rarely have occasion to interpose again, or to have his authority (as sometimes happens) supplemented by the vociferous calls of the majority to silence some otherwise irrepressible member.

In Congress the Order of Business is prescribed by the standing rules adopted and

amended from time to time by each House.
The standing rules of the Senate, as largely
changed and simplified in 1884, embrace forty
rules. The first business in order daily (after
prayer by the Chaplain) is reading the journal
of the preceding day. This can not be dispensed with unless by unanimous consent; any
mistake in .the journal may then be corrected,
on motion. Next, the President must lay before
the Senate Presidential messages, and reports
and communications from heads of departments, or other sources; also, bills and other
messages from the House of Representatives.
It is then in order for Senators to present:
(1) petitions and memorials for reference; (2)
reports of committees; (3) bills and resolutions.
These several classes of business occupy what
is called the morning hour, and until it is con-
cluded, no motion can be entertained by the
Chair, unless by unanimous consent. At the
conclusion of the morning business, the calendar of bills and resolutions is to be proceeded
with until 2 P. M., unless otherwise ordered;
bills not objected to are taken up in their order,
each Senator being entitled to speak once only

for five minutes on any question. At 2 o'clock, or earlier, if consideration of bills not objected to on the calendar is completed, special orders come up. If there be no special order, the calendar of general orders or unfinished business is proceeded with, occupying usually the remainder of the session. This order, however, yields to the following motions, if carried by a majority vote: (1) to proceed to the consideration of executive business; (2) to take up a revenue or appropriation bill; (3) to proceed to consider any other bill on the calendar; (4) to pass over the pending subject (which leaves it in its place for after-consideration); (5) to place the pending subject at the foot of the calendar. All these motions must be decided without debate. Special orders may be made at any time for a future day by a two-thirds vote; and they take precedence of all except the unfinished business of the preceding day, when the time fixed for their consideration arrives. Messages from the President or the House may be received during any proceeding, except while the Senate is dividing, or the journal is being read, or a question of order or adjournment is

pending. Reports of Committees of Conference have the same privilege. All reports of
committees as well as bills or resolutions offered
by individual Senators, must lie over one day,
unless otherwise directed by unanimous consent.
Bills and resolutions reported by committees are
to be placed on the calendar in their order.

The rules of the House of Representatives
differ in many respects from those of the Senate, and much more time is there consumed in
the raising, discussion and decision of points of
order. The prescribed Order of Business in
the House is: (1) prayer by the Chaplain; (2)
reading of the journal of the last day's sitting;
(3) the calling of the various committees, in
their order, to present reports. To this, what
is called the morning hour is devoted, except
on Mondays, when bills and resolutions are
presented, through a regular call of States, in
alphabetical order; (4) the unfinished business of the preceding session; (5) motions to
proceed to business on the Speaker's table;
(6) motions to go into Committee of the Whole
House upon revenue or appropriation bills;
(7) business on the House calendar, embracing

all public bills, except appropriation and revenue measures. The above order, however, is always subject to the privileged bills reported by the Committees of Ways and Means, Appropriations, Elections, Printing, Enrolled Bills, and Accounts.

Owing to the large number of Representatives (now 325 members, besides eight Territorial delegates), and to the enormous quantity of bills and resolutions offered, there is a slender chance for the consideration of the greater part of the legislation proposed to the House. Hence, comes a continual contest over the Order of Business, whenever bills having precedence from privileged committees are not under consideration. It requires a two-thirds majority to suspend the rules prescribing the regular Order of Business. As no motion to suspend the rules can be made, except on the first and third Monday of each month, and during the last six days of the session, this majority is rarely obtained. Special orders are, however, occasionally made in advance for given days by the requisite two-thirds vote. These special orders take precedence of all business, except revenue and appropriation bills, and the unfinished business of the day preceding. Questions of the priority of business must, under the rules, be decided by a majority, without debate. While any measure may be considered, by unanimous consent, this consent is comparatively rarely obtained.

In Parliament the Order of Business is regulated by appointing certain days to consider the orders of the day, and other days for original motions. To determine the order of offering the latter, the Speaker draws the names of members from a box; if present, they then rise and make their motions, without debate. Special orders are often appointed in advance. Government orders (*i. e.*, supply bills and other measures of the Ministry), are privileged on every order day except Wednesday, and on Friday the permanent order of the day is either bills of supply or ways and means. Every Wednesday is devoted to bills offered by members of the House not connected with the Ministry, unless overruled by pressing public business.

In the French Chamber of Deputies the Order

of Business for the next session is fixed by the body each day before adjourning, and this order is posted in the hall and published every morning in the *Journal Officiel*. This is an obvious advantage.

CHAPTER V

Officers.

To THE officers of an assembly, whether formally elected in pursuance of law or constitution, or more informally chosen for the purposes of a single meeting, belongs much power and corresponding responsibility. Upon their competence, impartiality, and knowledge of parliamentary law depend, in a large degree, the good order of the assembly, and the successful accomplishment of the business for which it is convened.

The presiding officer of every assembly is variously designated as the President, the Chairman, the Speaker, or the Moderator (the latter in some ecclesiastical bodies). While in legislative bodies the powers and duties of the presiding officer are closely defined by law or by the rules of the body, there is far more latitude allowed in less formal assemblies. Although the presiding officer is the head and to some extent the voice of the assembly, it should always be borne in mind that he is not the master but the

servant of the body which has elevated him to
the Chair. The highest function of a good
presiding officer is to ascertain and to carry
into effect the will of the assembly over which
he presides. At the same time, his decisions
are to be respected by all, unless in plain con-
flict with justice or well-recognized parliamentary rules. His service is best performed by preserving an even temper, a bearing toward the
members of mingled dignity and urbanity, a
prompt decision of questions of precedence
and order, and a close attention to debate, the
firm maintenance of order and the rights of the
minority as well as of the majority, and an impartial adherence to such parliamentary law as
is held to govern the body. It is the correlative
duty of the members to support the presiding
officer by orderly and respectful behavior, and
to treat him as the implicit organ of the assembly, entitled, by their assent in electing him,
to control the course of business and debate,
and to be the arbiter between opposing views
upon all questions as to the proper conduct of
the proceedings.

The presiding' officer should stand when

addressing the assembly, hearing or putting
motions, taking votes, or deciding any question.
During debate, the reading of reports or minutes, and at other times, he should occupy the
chair. In smaller or more informal meetings
(as of committees, societies. boards of managers, etc.,) the Chairman commonly sits through
the whole proceedings. When a member addresses the Chair, he should always say, "*Mr.
President*," or "*Mr. Chairman:*" and it is
usual, though not obligatory, for the Chairman
to recognize him by name or (in conventions)
as "*The gentleman from* ——." The presiding
officer and not the assembly is to be addressed
by all speakers. He may check irrelevant discussion by confining debate to the subject before the body. In deciding points of order, he
may give his reasons or not, at his pleasure. The
proper form, when he rules out the point of
order. is: "The Chair overrules the point of
order;" when he admits it: "The point of order
is well taken," or "The Chair sustains the point
of order."

The place of the presiding officer, in case of
his absence, is filled by a Vice-President or a

President *pro tempore*, in case such an officer exists; if not, the assembly elects a temporary Chairman. The Chair has the right to call another member to take his place, if he desires to participate in debate; but it is better, for obvious reasons, that he should avoid anything like partisanship. The Chair has the right to vote in all cases of ballot, like other members, but in voting by division of the assembly, or by ayes and noes, he can vote only in case of a tie.

In the Senate of the United States, the Constitution makes the Vice-President the presiding officer. In his absence, a President *pro tempore* must be chosen. In either case, the presiding officer has the right to name any Senator to perform the duties of the Chair, but this substitution cannot extend beyond an adjournment. He may decide questions of order, subject to appeal to the Senate; or, at his option, he may submit any question of order for the decision of the Senate. He has no power to appoint standing committees, but appoints committees of conference between the two Houses, on motion and concurrence of the body, and is usually authorized by the Senate to fill vacancies in the regular committees.

In the House of Representatives, the presiding officer is called the Speaker, a term derived from the British Parliament. The name imports that he is the mouthpiece or organ of the body, and is to announce its will. His salary is $8,000, while that of other members of the House is $5,000. The duties of the Speaker, as laid down in the rules of the House of Representatives, involve the exercise of very great powers. He appoints the chairmen and members of all standing and select committees, preserves order and decorum in the House, states all questions, decides points of order, recognizes or declines to recognize members to speak or to offer motions, enforces the rules, signs all acts, resolutions and processes of the House, appoints its official reporters and the stenographers of committees, and has general control of the hall of the House, etc. The Speaker is not required to vote except in certain cases of a tie, or when a vote is taken by ballot. He has always the right, however, to vote as a Representative, but seldom exercises it except on very important questions. The Speaker may appoint any member to perform the duties of the Chair *pro tempore* (which power is limited to ten days), but if absent without having made such appointment, the House must elect a Speaker *pro tempore*, who is addressed as *"Mr. Speaker."* The Speaker may call any member to preside when leaving the chair temporarily, and this member is addressed as *"Mr. Chairman."* When the House goes into the Committee of the Whole, the Speaker designates a member to preside, relinquishing his seat, and this member is addressed as *"Mr. Chairman."* When, by motion and vote, the Committee of the Whole agree to rise (which means, simply, reconverting the body into the House without leaving their seats), the Speaker resumes the chair, and the Chairman of the Committee of the Whole formally reports to him what business has been under consideration, and whether any action or conclusion has been reached thereon.

The Speaker uses a gavel in rapping the House to order. The mace, which is brought in and placed at the Speaker's right on the

assembling of the House, is the time-honored
emblem of popular sovereignty as represented
in the Legislature. There is no mace in the
Senate nor in the House of Lords. The mace
used in the House is in the form of a carved .
and gilded block about three feet high, repre-
senting the Roman *fasces*, with ebony base,
silver bands and spears, topped by a globe of
silver bearing an eagle with half-spread wings.
When the House is in Committee of the Whole
the mace is removed by the Sergeant-at-Arms.

In Parliament the Speaker of the House of
Lords is the Lord High Chancellor. He has
no casting vote, and if the Lords are evenly
divided the question is lost. He may leave the
chair and speak in his character of a peer.
The Speaker of the House of Commons is
elected by the members at the beginning of
each new Parliament. He wears a full-bot-
tomed wig and black silk robes, and enters the
House of Commons with much ceremony, pre-
ceded by the mace, and followed by a Train-
bearer, Chaplain and Secretary. The Speaker
cannot participate in debate, but has the cast-

ing vote in case of a tie in the House of Commons.

Next in importance to the presiding officer
of any assembly is the recording officer, known
as the Secretary or Clerk. It is his function to
keep the record of proceedings, minutes or
journal. This he commonly reads, by direction
of the presiding officer, at the meeting next
succeeding that which it covers. The Secretary's minutes should embrace every motion or
resolution (with names of the movers) with the
action thereon, whether adopted, amended, rejected or otherwise disposed of; also, the names
of the presiding officer and Secretary, time and
place of meeting, etc. In societies, these minutes sometimes embrace, also, a record of members present, or participating in discussion, or
reading papers. The Secretary is the custodian
of all record books and papers of the assembly,
and should keep an order of business, with a
list of all committees, reports, adjournments,
votes, orders, elections, etc. In permanent
societies, whether literary, scientific or charita-
ble, and in ecclesiastical bodies, it is customary
to have both a Recording Secretary and a Cor-

responding Secretary, the latter to conduct communications with other organizations or individuals. In conventions, and some other public meetings, it is usual to appoint one or more assistant Secretaries, or a stenographer, so that a full record, or sometimes a *verbatim* report may be kept for publication.

The Secretary of any body should not incorporate in his minutes any opinions or criticisms, laudatory or otherwise, as to the discussions or papers read; he is not there as a censor or judge of merit, but as a simple recorder of things done. Any statement in the minutes, if deemed erroneous, may be questioned by any member, and, on motion, changed by the assembly. The Secretary is to read all papers called for (except the contributions of individual members, or reports, which may be read by the author or the chairman of the committee reporting them), call the roll of members when required, collect ballots, aid the President in his duties, issue notices of meetings, announcements to members or others, of special action, etc. In the absence of the President or his substitute, he should call the meeting to order, and nominate, or call for nominations, of a presiding officer. He should sign the minutes, and certify (with the President, when required), to any record of the proceedings of the assembly. His records should be always open to the inspection of members.

In Congress, the recording officer of the Senate is called the Secretary, while in the House he is styled the Clerk. These officers have responsible custody of all files of papers (public and private), bills, petitions, etc., which accumulate in the course of the business of the Senate and House. They must, in person or by their assistants, note all questions of order and decisions thereon; keep the journals of the respective Houses, and print them in well-indexed volumes; publicly read all bills, resolutions, motions. etc., brought before the respective Houses; attest, by their signature (and sometimes by seal of the Senate or House), all bills, resolutions, writs, warrants and subpœnas; disburse the contingent fund, and make contracts for supplies, labor, stationery, etc. All messages from one House to the other are conveyed and announced *viva voce* to the presiding

officer by this functionary or one of his assistants.
Besides these duties, the Secretary of the Senate is charged with paying the salaries of members, and calls the Senate to order, in the absence of any presiding officer, until a President
pro tem. is designated. The Clerk of the House
continues in office until the organization of the
House succeeding that which elected him. It
is his duty to call the new House to order, call
the roll of members, and to preside, and determine all questions of order until a Speaker is
elected, subject to an appeal to the House.
His successor is chosen by *viva voce* vote as
soon as the Speaker is elected.

In most permanent societies, a Treasurer is
an essential adjunct of the official organization.
In small bodies the Secretary often acts as
Treasurer also. The function of the Treasurer
is to receive and disburse all moneys belonging
to the society, whether as members' dues or
otherwise, keeping account in detail in a book
provided for the purpose. Customarily, the
Treasurer pays out money only upon vouchers,
attested by the President or the Secretary, or
both. He makes an annual report of all these

transactions, which is usually audited by a committee appointed by the Chair, and their report of correctness should be accepted by the society, thus relieving the disbursing officer of responsibility up to a given date.

In conventions, it is usual to appoint, in addition to the other officers, a Sergeant-at-Arms or Doorkeeper, who has charge of the entrance to the place of meeting, and whose duty it is to aid the Chair at all times in preserving order, and to be ready to assist the members in any needed arrangements or communications. He should have the power to appoint such assistants as may be needed in order to the efficient discharge of these duties.

In the Senate, the Sergeant-at-Arms is elected by the body, and is required to attend its sittings, to maintain order and decorum, to serve processes, and make arrests, when required by the presiding officer, and to take absent members into custody and bring them to the hall, upon a call of the House. The Sergeant-at-Arms of the House, besides being charged with all these duties, pays the salaries of the members. The Doorkeeper of the House is an elective officer, who has charge of the hall, its entrances, committee-rooms and public property therein, announces messages at the door of the House, and is responsible for the strict enforcement of the rules regarding admission to the floor. He has the appointment of a large number of messengers, assistant doorkeepers and pages. The Sergeant-at-Arms of the Senate appoints the Doorkeeper and his assistants in that body.

CHAPTER VI

Committees.

THE function of committees in deliberative assemblies is to economize time and systematize business. A committee brings together in a few presumably competent hands, the preparation of business for the action of the whole body, which might otherwise consume much time in crude and contradictory attempts at discussion or expression. One or more subjects may thus be referred to one or more committees, according to the pleasure of the body. In conventions it is customary to appoint: (1) a Committee on Permanent Officers; (2) a Committee on Credentials or Elections; (3) a Committee on Rules, or the Order of Business; (4) a Committee on Resolutions; and such other committees as convenience or the objects of the assembly may require; *e. g.*, on admission to the hall, on invitations, etc. The motion to appoint a committee may come from any member. The Chair then puts the question: " Is it your pleasure that such a committee be ap-

pointed?" If carried, the Chair inquires:
"How- shall the committee be appointed?"
when it is usual to move that the presiding
officer appoint, although the motion may
be that the Chair nominate the committee to
the assembly, which may then confirm or re-
ject the nomination. If the number of which
the committee shall consist is not stated in the
motion, the Chair should put the question:
"How many shall constitute the committee?"
and it is usual to name three, five, seven or more
as the number of members; always an odd
number, that they may not be evenly divided,
and so unable to agree on a report. It is also
usual, though by no means an invariable custom, for the Chair to appoint the mover as chairman of the committee. A small committee of
three members is, in most cases, much better than
a larger number, as leading to less debate and
more prompt dispatch of business. Committees on resolutions, however, and other committees in large conventions, where the honor
of selection counts for much, are usually made
quite large; as in National conventions, one
from each State represented. In appointing

committees, where there are known differences
of opinion as to matters to be considered by
them, care should be taken to appoint members
from all parties, while the majority of the committee should consist of friends of the measure
referred to them, or of the party known to be
dominant in the assembly.

By established custom the first person named
on a committee is its chairman; but the committee may think proper to elect another chairman, and this right cannot be contested except
when the law governing the assembly explicitly
invests the presiding officer with power to appoint the chairman (as in the House of Representatives).

The committee being appointed, the member
named as chairman should be furnished by the
Secretary with a copy of the resolution of appointment, the matter referred to them, with
any instructions, and the names of the members. A majority of the committee constitutes
a quorum. They should be convened by the
chairman, who should state the exact business
referred to them, reading any papers committed.
If resolutions are referred, the committee should

consider them in their order, amending them at
pleasure; or if the committee are to bring in
resolutions of their own, it is usual for a member
or a sub-committee to be agreed upon to draft
them, after which the chairman may call for
amendments *seriatim*. The amendments offered
being adopted or rejected, the chairman calls
for a vote upon the entire report. If the committee think proper to change resolutions referred to them, they are to report them back
intact, with a substitute, or with their amendments proposed separately.

If a portion of the members cannot agree
with the majority, they may submit a minority
report. When the business before the committee is finished, it is usual to move that the
chairman, or another member conversant with
the subject, report their action to the assembly. The report is then opened to the whole
body for discussion, in which it is not parliamentary for any one to refer to what has passed
in committee. It is unnecessary, although
quite frequently done, to move that a report be
received, its reading being sufficient evidence of
its reception. The motion to accept a report

is equivalent to adopting it, or to agree to it as the sense of the assembly. This motion should never be put by the Chair until he has called for remarks upon the question. When a committee report has been made to the assembly, the committee becomes *functus officio*, unless a standing committee of the body. If, however, the report is recommitted, the committee will again act. When the report of a committee is adopted or agreed to, it becomes thereby the act of the assembly. In conventions or other assemblies, during the absence of a committee to prepare business, the time may be devoted to debate or to motions regarding other business. After the reading of a committee's report, the minority report, if any, is in order for presentation; and a motion can be made to substitute it for the report of the committee.

In Congress, the power and practical utility of committees, in giving form to all business before the body, can hardly be overrated. In fact, so powerful are the recommendations of some leading committees, that it may fairly be said that the committees, and not Congress, make the laws. Congressional committees are of four kinds: standing committees, select or special committees, committees of conference, and committees of the whole house. A member may be appointed to act upon as many as three standing committees, or upon one only.

In the Senate, the standing committees are appointed at the commencement of each Congress, and they are thirty-eight in number (in 1884). The method of appointing members of committees (unlike that in the House, where the Speaker has uncontrolled power to appoint), is for a caucus of the party having a majority in the Senate to select, by agreement, the chairmen and the majority of each committee, leaving the minority to be named by the caucus of the party which is in the minority in the Senate. The rule provides that the chairman of each committee shall be appointed by ballot in open Senate, unless otherwise ordered; after which all the other members of the committees must be appointed by one ballot. In practice, however, the chairman of the caucus of the party having a majority moves that the rule requiring a ballot be suspended, and that the list of committees be constituted as in the paper submitted; and this motion is, by unanimous consent, agreed to. In the choice of a chairman of a standing committee, a majority of the whole number of votes given is necessary, but a plurality of votes may elect the other members. All other committees are appointed by plurality, and by ballot, unless otherwise ordered. Vacancies in committees are customarily filled by the presiding officer, who must, however, be specially authorized by the Senate. The Senate committees consist of different numbers, varying from three to eleven members each. Each standing Senate committee has a committee-room assigned to it, and a clerk to record its proceedings, call meetings, etc. Select committees are such as are appointed to consider and report upon special subjects not considered as permanently before the body.

In the House of Representatives, the Speaker appoints all committees, both standing and select, with their chairmen, for the Congress, or for two years. The House standing committees number forty-seven, three of which are joint committees, empowered to act with similar committees of the Senate. They consist of numbers varying from three up to fifteen members each, the greater number having eleven members. Of late, Territorial delegates have been placed upon certain standing committees, with the same power they have in the House, to speak but not to vote. Select committees, ordered by the House from time to time to report upon special subjects, do not hold over the session, unless specially authorized. The meetings of committees are private, unless they prefer to admit spectators, but any member of Congress may at any time appear before them, and it is usual to give a hearing to the promoters of any interest related to the subjects before them, and such hearings are generally public. Each committee has a clerk appointed by the chairman, if the committee approve, and a docket or calendar of business. Some committees, having constantly important business, meet daily, some weekly, and many occasionally, or upon call of the chairman. The chairman of any committee may legally administer oaths to witnesses. The House sometimes grants special power to committees to send for persons and papers, to

sit in the recess of Congress, or in any part of
the country, and to sit during sessions of the
House. All reports made by committees must
be written, and when the rules give the committee the right to report at any time, this involves the right to consider the matter when
reported. Reports may be made by the chairman, or by any designated member of the committee; and when the report is considered, the
one making it has the right to open and close
debate thereon. Minority reports are commonly printed just after the report of the
majority, so that they may be considered there-
with. There is a call of the committees daily
for reports, except on the first and third Monday of each month. Committees are frequently at variance upon questions of jurisdiction
or proper reference of certain measures; these
controversies are decided by the Speaker or the
House, on the theory that the principal subject of the bill governs its reference.

In the British Parliament, the only standing·
committees are those on Accounts, Standing
Orders, Selection, and Railway Bills; these must
be re-appointed each session. Select commit-

tees are appointed either by ballot or *viva voce*, on motion of any member naming them. The quorum of the committee (usually numbering fifteen) is fixed by the House, and is commonly three members in the Lords and five in the Commons. Committee sessions are usually open, though strangers may be excluded at any time, and this is done while the committee are deliberating. All evidence is taken in shorthand and printed. In 1883 a new rule was adopted in the Commons, constituting several " grand committees," for the purpose of giving thorough consideration to all important measures before presenting them in Parliament for debate. This object has been well accomplished hitherto, increasing the working power of the Parliament.

In the French Chamber of Deputies, the Committee on the Budget is the most important, having thirty-three members, charged with all legislation involving revenue and expenditure. No member can be appointed to more than two committees. One day weekly is usually set apart for committee work.

Committee of the Whole.

The Committee of the Whole House is formed for the consideration of some specific business, and is constituted of all the individual members of the body. By the rules of the House of Representatives, all bills making appropriations, or relating to revenue, must first be considered in Committee of the Whole. When the motion is made and carried to go into Committee of the Whole, the Speaker appoints a chairman to preside, and leaves the chair. Business is proceeded with in the order of the calendar, unless the House goes into committee on a specific bill. Speeches are limited to five minutes for each side on any amendment offered; but *pro forma* amendments (to strike out the last word, etc.), greatly extend this limit as to the number of speeches. When debate runs too long, it is not cut off by the committee, but those in charge of the measure move that the committee rise; and the Speaker resuming the chair, the House is asked to adopt a motion closing debate on the pending section. This, if carried, stops debate, but does not bar out other amendments. If messages to the House come in, or other business requires the immediate attention of the House, the committee rise, and the Speaker resumes the chair; after the matter is disposed of, the House again resolves itself into committee. All divisions in Committee of the Whole are taken either by the sound—aye or no—or by a rising vote; or, when these are unsatisfactory, by tellers. The yeas and nays cannot be called in committee, nor can any motions to reconsider, or to lay on the table, or to order the previous question, be made. But any member may reserve the right to have a separate vote in the House upon any clause or amendment. When the business under deliberation in committee is completed, the committee rise and the chairman reports to the Speaker: "The Committee of the Whole House on the state of the Union, having had under consideration (such a subject), have directed me to report the same, with amendments."

In the Senate, the body does not formally resolve itself into Committee of the Whole, but simply adopts an order that the business pending shall be considered "as in Committee of the

Whole." This is called by Mr. Jefferson a *quasi* committee. The rule requires all bills and joint resolutions to be considered first as in Committee of the Whole, before being reported to the Senate; and any amendments made in committee must again be considered by the Senate, when other amendments may be proposed.

In the British Parliament, instead of calling any member to the chair, the Committee of the Whole is presided over by the chairman of the Ways and Means in the House of Commons, and in the House of Lords by the chairman of committees appointed each session. The function of committees of the whole House is deliberation. All public bills, and whatever relates to religion, trade, revenue or money grants, are first considered in Committee of the Whole.

Committees of Conference.

Committees of Conference between the two Houses are appointed by the presiding officer of each, to adjust differences upon a measure which has passed both Houses, though in a different form. These conference committees embrace three members from each House, two of whom are of the majority party, or in favor of the measure. The form of moving a conference, when either House non-concurs with the amendments to any measure made by the other, is "that the House (or Senate) insist on its disagreement and ask for a conference." The opposite motion (sometimes, though rarely, carried) is that the House (or Senate) recede from its amendments, or from its disagreement, and agree to the amendments of the other body. If the conferees fail to agree, they so report to their respective Houses, and a new committee is moved, or the same is re-appointed. Three or four conferences, with as many committees, are not infrequent. The report of a Conference Committee must be signed by a majority of the committee of both Houses, and its presentation is always in order. The Senate rule requires the question on considering a conference report to be determined without debate. The Committee of Conference may be instructed by a vote of either House, but its report cannot be amended or altered like those of other committees. It is usual, after a second disagreement between the conferees, for them to state the points of disagreement in making their report.

In Parliament, Conference Committees are of more formal consequence, business being suspended in both Houses during their sittings. They may be demanded by either House, to consider the privileges of Parliament, the course of proceeding, and the bills or amendments passed by the other. Managers are appointed by the Commons and by the Lords, and both Houses are thus brought, by deputations of their own members, into direct intercourse with each other.

In the French legislative body, when the Senate and the Chamber of Deputies disagree, a Committee of Conference may be moved, to agree upon a new form of the bill in controversy. If the conference report is rejected, however, by the Deputies (or lower House), it is not in order to bring in a similar bill until two months have expired, unless at the initiative of the government.

CHAPTER VII

Rules.

PERMANENT or elective bodies are generally governed by systematic rules. Most societies have their constitutions and by-laws, either written or printed, which prescribe the action of the body, define the powers and duties of the officers, and settle many questions that arise, without recourse to parliamentary law. A constitution should be as simple and direct as possible, and should leave no room for controversy as to the meaning of its various articles. It is usual to provide in the body of a constitution (by articles and sections duly numbered) for the organization, membership, officers, meetings, finances, etc., of the society. Every constitution should contain provision for its own amendment. It is customary, in order to avoid too great facility of change by a mere majority, to insert a provision that two-thirds of the whole number of members (or two-thirds of those present) shall be required to adopt

68

amendments to the constitution, and this only at regular stated meetings, after a specific notice.

The by-laws following a constitution should embrace all necessary details, except such as are left to the officers, under generally recognized usages of parliamentary law. The standing Rules of Order of the society, such as are not to be changed at the will of any meeting, are embodied in the by-laws, or may form a supplement thereto. The by-laws, like the constitution, should be amendable only by a two-thirds vote, after due previous notice. In framing and adopting a constitution and by-laws, a committee is appointed to draft them and report at an adjourned meeting. When reported, the presiding officer should read each article separately, and call for any proposed amendments thereto; after which he should take the vote—first, upon amendments in their order, and then upon the article itself. The whole having been gone through with, additional amendments are in order, after which the vote should be taken on the adoption of the whole constitution as amended. The question on amending and adopting the by-laws should be taken separately. It is usual for the members present to sign the constitution, and for members subsequently elected under its provisions to do the same. A provision is usually inserted for suspending the rules or by-laws by vote of two-thirds of the members present. Without such provision, the course of business they prescribe must be strictly adhered to.

In parliamentary bodies, what are known as the Standing Rules are of great importance. They should contain, in the most clear and succinct form of statement, the prescribed method of procedure in every contingency not regulated by legal or constitutional provisions. These latter, indeed, are frequently repeated in the rules as adopted by a legislative body. The present Standing Rules of the Senate, as amended to March 24, 1884, are clearly set forth in forty rules, some of which have from two to five clauses. They prescribe the order and method of conducting business in the Senate, and their enforcement can be suspended only by unanimous consent of the Senate. No motion to amend any rule is in order, except on one day's notice in writing, specifying the rule to be amended, and the purpose thereof.

The Standing Rules of the House of Representatives received their latest thorough revision in the year 1880. They embrace forty-five distinct rules, and provide that these shall be the rules of each Congress, unless otherwise ordered. To Thomas Jefferson's " Manual of Parliamentary Practice," first published in 1801, and still made a part of every reprint of the House Manual, we are indebted for the first Rules of Parliamentary Law ever put into systematic form in America. These rules still govern the House, where they are applicable and not inconsistent with the Standing Rules adopted. The standing Committee on Rules consists of five members, of whom the Speaker forms one. To them is referred all proposed action touching the rules or procedure of the body. Several struggles have occurred between parties, involving the application or radical change of the rules. The last of these, in the Forty-seventh Congress, called out a decision from the Speaker that no dilatory motions to obstruct the adoption or amendment of rules of procedure could be entertained. This decision was rested upon the ground that, as the Constitution explicitly confers upon the House the right to determine its own rules, a majority of that body must, at all times, have the power to make or to alter rules, independently of the existing ones.

The motion to suspend the rules is designed to make some business in order which would not be regularly so under their restrictions. This suspension always requires a vote of two-thirds of the members present. It must first be seconded by a majority, counted by tellers, if demanded, and the motion is debatable for half an hour only. A suspension of the rules can be moved in the House only upon the first and third Monday of each month, or else during the last six days of a session.

However rigid and binding the rules governing an assembly may be, they can always be suspended by unanimous consent. This is sometimes obtained to accomplish, without delay, an object greatly desired by the vast majority, if not by all of the body.

The rules of the Senate provide for special

orders to consider any subject, for which a day
may be fixed in advance by vote of two-thirds
of the Senators present. When 2 o'clock of
the day arrives, unfinished business of the preceding day takes precedence of the special
order. When a special order is not finally disposed of on the day set for it, it resumes its
place at the head of the calendar of special
orders, unless it becomes unfinished business by
adjournment. All motions to change special
orders must be decided by the majority without
debate. In the House, a special order can be
made only by unanimous consent, or by vote
of two-thirds, on either of the two days in each
month when suspension of the rules is in order. In making special orders, it is usual to
insert the proviso, " not to interfere with general appropriation or revenue bills." Special
orders are frequently made for more than one
subject, by assigning a day to a committee for
the consideration of such business as it may
present. When the time fixed for a special
order arrives, it takes precedence of all other
business until disposed of, with such exception
as may have been reserved in the order itself.

(3)

An important rule of the House of Representatives provides that all questions regarding the priority of business shall be decided by a majority without debate. Another rule sets apart every Friday for the consideration of private business, unless two-thirds of the members voting determine otherwise.

All business undisposed of at the end of any Congress falls with the Congress, whether bills, reports, or matters unagreed to between the two Houses. But all business undisposed of at the close of any session, except the final one, is by a rule of each House resumed, and is in order for action in the same manner as if no adjournment had taken place. The same committees also resume control of all matters referred to them and undisposed of at the preceding session. Papers referred to Senate committees must be deposited during the recess of Congress in the office of the Secretary of the Senate. There they remain among the files, unless the next session is one of the same Congress, in which case they are to be returned to the several committees to which they had previously been referred. This last provision is a

Standing Rule of the Senate; in the House, papers referred to standing committees usually remain in the committee-rooms from the close of one session to the next convening of the same Congress, though the rule requires the Clerk to take custody of all such files at the expiration of the Congress.

The rules of the two Houses, although having a certain general similarity, differ materially in many points regulating the conduct of business. (1) In the Senate, petitions and memorials are presented in open session during the morning hour, and publicly referred to committees. In the House of Representatives, petitions are no longer (since 1853) presented publicly, but are handed to the Clerk for such reference as the member having them in charge endorses thereon. In either case a brief statement of the petitions and memorials is entered on the journal, and published daily in the *Congressional Record*. (2) Private bills have every Friday set apart for their consideration in the House, unless otherwise determined by a two-thirds vote; but there is no special day for private bills in the Senate. (3) In the Senate, bills cannot be offered without one day's notice, unless by unanimous consent. In the House, any member may offer bills without limit, but on Mondays only, unless unanimous consent is obtained. (4) Debate in the House is restricted by the rules within very narrow lines: first, by limiting set speeches to one hour; secondly, by limiting debate on amendments and the details of measures to five-minute speeches; thirdly, by providing for the previous question (the effect of which is to close debate) being called by a majority at any time. The Senate has no one-hour rule, no previous question, and no limitation of debate, except when considering business on the calendar, when each Senator is limited to one speech and to five minutes only.

In the British Parliament, the rules are known as Standing Orders. These are frequently revised, but continue from one Parliament to another, unless modified. These Standing Orders of the Lords and of the Commons, together with the orders for proceedings upon private bills, are frequently reprinted.

In the French Chamber of Deputies, the

rules are embodied in a code embracing 154
articles. Any question of order, or appeal to
the rules, suspends discussion, and has precedence over any other business before the body.

Joint Rules.

Joint Rules are those which have been
agreed to by both houses of a parliamentary
body. They relate to the conduct of business
between the two Houses. As early as 1790 several Joint Rules were adopted by the Senate and
House, and were continued in force until the
Forty-fourth Congress. By far the most important of these was the 22d Joint Rule, regulating
the counting of the votes for President and
Vice-President, when the two Houses convened
in joint session for that purpose. In January,
1876, the majority in the two Houses being of
opposite politics, the Senate sent to the House
a concurrent resolution adopting as the Joint
Rules for that session the series of such rules
previously in force, except the 22d. The
House took no action upon this, and the Senate, shortly before the adjournment in August,
1876, passed a resolution to notify the House

that, as that body had not notified the Senate
of the adoption of the Joint Rules as proposed
by the Senate, there were no Joint Rules in force.
This left the Presidential count unregulated by
any joint rule, and the disputed Presidential
election of November, 1876, intervening, Congress passed the Electoral Commission bill
(approved January 29, 1877), prescribing that
the votes should be counted at the joint session
of the two Houses, as determined by the majority of the Electoral Commission. This, however, prescribed the rule for that election only.
At the next Presidential count (in February,
1881), the two Houses had to pass a special
concurrent resolution regulating their meeting
and the count of the vote, in the absence of any
law or rule (other than the Constitution) on the
subject.

CHAPTER VIII

Questions.

ALL business which comes before a deliberative body or a public assembly may be termed a question. To determine the sense of the assembly upon the question is the ultimate aim toward which all preliminary machinery, motions, resolutions, debate, amendments, points of order, rulings, appeals, etc., steadily tend. Amid the apparently intricate heaping of rules upon rules, and the sad consumption of valuable time upon futile points of order and contradictory discussions, it is not singular to find the average mind puzzled and full of uncertainty. What is required, but too seldom found, in the application of parliamentary law to the business in hand, is simplicity instead of intricacy, and an assured standard of appeal, instead of a mixture of often conflicting decisions. Hence the great importance of the adoption of some systematic rules which shall govern at least the general course of procedure, fix the order of motions, limit the latitude of debate, and conduce toward a prompt if not quite satisfactory settlement of every controverted question through the decision of the Chair, or by the will of the majority. As no system of rules can alone be trusted to effect this result, without the constant aid of a firm, skillful and courteous presiding officer to enforce them, so no presiding officer, on the other hand, can forward the business of a large and often inharmonious body to a successful result, without constant reliance upon some recognized code of procedure. While the decisions of the Chairman are always subject to the test of an appeal to the assembly, experience proves that time wasted in taking such questions, obstructs the business of the body, and is not compensated by the supposed advantage of establishing a principle.

The term Motion is used to designate every proposition submitted by a member of an assembly. It is a rule without an exception, that no one can address the Chair or the meeting except to make a motion of some kind, or to speak upon a motion of some kind already before the body. In ordinary assemblies, mo-

tions made by any one member are to be
seconded by some other member before being
voted upon; but no second is required in Congress. Every motion must be reduced to writing if any member demands it, and should then
be placed in the hands of the President, who
refers it to the Secretary after the assembly has
come to a conclusion thereon. If a verbal or
informal motion, the presiding officer states it
to the assembly; if in writing, it is read by the
Chair, or by the Clerk. It is the duty of the
Chair, upon stating the motion, to put the question: "Is there a second?" after which he
states that it is moved and seconded, etc.,
repeating the motion. This brings the subject
of the motion formally before the assembly,
and of course beyond the control of the
mover for change, withdrawal, etc. The motion is now open to several courses of action
on the part of the assembly. They may choose
to debate it; to amend it; to adopt a substitute
for it; to refer it to a committee; to lay it upon
the table; to postpone it to a definite future
time; or, finally, to put it to vote for adoption
or rejection. A motion which, if carried, may

render any of these superfluous, is the motion
to postpone indefinitely. This motion, if made
and seconded as soon as the main motion is
properly before the assembly, cannot be amended, and comes up for immediate decision. If
carried, further consideration of the main question is defeated, and the original motion is lost
and cannot be renewed. If the motion for in-
definite postponement is lost, the original motion becomes again the pending business.

Adjournments.

In every deliberative body, the motion to adjourn has precedence of all others, and is not, at
least in American usage, subject to debate nor
amendment. It may be made at any time, although it cannot interrupt a member speaking,
nor the House when dividing; nor can it be
made when a similar motion has just been
negatived, though it is renewable after other
business has intervened. Unfinished business,
cut off by an adjournment, has precedence in
the orders of the day for the next session. The
Constitution restrains either House of Congress
from adjourning for more than three days to-

gether, without the concurrence of the other. If the Houses should disagree as to the time of adjournment, the President may, by the Constitution, adjourn them to such time as he may think proper; but this power has never been exercised.

In the British Parliament, the motion to adjourn is debatable, and it may be amended as to the time of adjournment. In the House of Commons, the Speaker must adjourn the House when he finds it without a quorum, if the fact is noted. In the French Legislative Corps, the President takes the sense of the Chamber, before each day's adjournment, as to the day and hour of the next meeting, as well as the measures to be considered.

Amendments.

Amendments to a motion are always in order, and one amendment to an amendment is also in order; but no motion to amend farther than this can be entertained. Subsidiary motions of all kinds are subject to the general rule that only one question can be considered at the same time. But if a dilatory motion, or a privileged one, or one ordering the main

question be made, it is held to supersede
motions to amend, as it may lead to such a
disposition of the question as would preclude
the necessity of amendment. There are three
principal ways of amending a motion: by in-
sertion of new matter, by omission, and by
substitution. All motions to amend should be,
like the original motion, in writing, and should
be carefully prepared and clearly expressed. If
rejected, the precise amendment defeated is not
again in order. Amendments once agreed to can
not afterward be altered or amended. Amendment by substitution is reached by a motion to
strike out and insert; and this motion, by the
rule of the House of Representatives, is indi-
visible. Amendments should be made in the
order of sequence. When the subject-matter
to be amended consists of several sections or
paragraphs, it is not in order to go back and
amend parts which have been already considered. In the House of Representatives, motions to amend may be withdrawn or modified
before the previous question is ordered, but not
afterward; and amendments so withdrawn may
be re-offered at a subsequent stage of the pro-

ceedings. Amendments are often proposed to defeat a proposition, as well as to advance its object; and the opponents of a motion often attempt its defeat by moving amendments or riders which render it objectionable or absurd. Such amendments may even reverse its purport or intent, so that the supporters of the original measure will join with its opponents to defeat it. If an amendment to strike out is adopted, it is not in order to move to insert the words stricken out in the same place, but they may be moved in a subsequent place. It is an invariable rule that motions to amend take precedence, and are properly considered before what it is proposed to amend, the question being first taken on the amendment. The same rule applies to an amendment of an amendment. No amendment can be in order which contravenes the law or the constitution, or the standing or special orders of the assembly, or which is identical with any proposition already voted upon during the same meeting. Much controversy has arisen as to whether amendments not germane to the subject under consideration can be admitted as in order. The

strong preponderance of authorities, however,
rules out any amendment on a subject different
from that under consideration. This is the ex-
plicit rule in the House of Representatives,
which reads: " No motion or proposition on
a subject different from that under consideration shall be admitted under cover of amendment." The Senate has no such general rule,
but has the following as to amendments to appropriation bills : " Nor shall any amendments
not germane or relevant to the subject-matter
contained in the bill be received; nor shall any
amendment to any item or clause of such bill
be received which does not directly relate
thereto; and all questions of relevancy of
amendments shall be decided without debate."
The rule in Parliament is, that an amendment
must be coherent and consistent with the con-
text of the bill; and an amendment made by
one House to an amendment made by the
other, must be relevant to the same subject-
matter. An amendment to strike out is put
directly in this country, but the opposite rule
prevails in Parliament, the Speaker putting the
question whether the words proposed to be

stricken out shall stand. A member may move
to substitute a wholly different proposition for
the one moved, except in Committee of the
Whole House, which is authorized only to consider the subject referred to it. In Congress,
debate upon amendments is limited to five minutes for each speaker in Committee of the
Whole, but the majority may, at any time, close
all debate upon any pending amendment; after
which further amendments may be offered, to
be decided without debate. Amendments do
not require a second in either House of Congress; but in the House of Commons, every
amendment must be proposed and seconded,
the same as an original motion. In Congress,
no amendment is in order to an appropriation
bill which adds to expenditure, or which
changes existing law. Amendments, however,
which retrench expenditure and are germane to
the subject-matter, may be entertained in the
House, although they may alter the law. Any
bill passed by one House is subject to amendment in all its parts by the other. When returned to the other body, the motion is usually
made to non-concur in the amendments as a

whole, and appoint a Committee of Conference. No bill can be amended after both Houses have agreed to it.

Appeal.

All decisions of the presiding officer of an assembly are made subject to an appeal to the body itself. An appeal is often taken from a ruling of the Chairman on a point of order, and this may be moved by the member whom the Chair has overruled, or by any member. Appeals are debatable, and it is usual for the Chair to state the ground of his ruling, pending the question on the appeal. If any member appeals from the Chair's decision, and the appeal is seconded, the question is put by the presiding officer: "Shall the decision of the Chair stand as the judgment of the body?" If the decision is not sustained, the Chair is overruled by a majority of the members, and such a decision stands as a precedent of some importance on similar questions that may arise. Frequently the motion is made to lay the appeal on the table, which, if carried, has the effect to sustain the decision of the Chair. In Congress, a rule of the House requires that

the Speaker shall decide questions of order
subject to an appeal by any member, and this
appeal is debatable, except after a motion for
the previous question. The Senate rule requires
that questions of order be decided by the presiding officer, unless submitted by him to the
Senate; such questions must be decided without debate, subject to an appeal. The appeal
may be laid on the table, and thereupon the action of the Senate is held as affirming the decision of the President. The presiding officer of an
assembly may give his reasons for the decision
which leads to the appeal, without leaving the
Chair. Unless a standing rule prevents, an appeal is debatable, no one member, however,
speaking more than once. Questions of order
once decided on appeal, cannot be renewed at
the same sitting.

In Parliament, no appeal is provided for, but
the Speaker of the Lords, as well as of the Commons, refers questions of order for the most
part directly to the decision of the House.

Attendance.

The presence in an assembly of all regular
members is assumed to be due to their constitu-

ents, at least in representative bodies. In conventions held for a specific purpose, where delegates are elected, it is usual to elect, also, alternates or proxies, to take the place of the regularly elected delegates, should occasion arise.
The alternates may or may not attend the convention, although in most cases they are present.
In legislative bodies, no alternate, substitute or
proxy can take the place of a member elect,
though voting by proxy was allowed in the
British House of Lords until 1868, when the
practice was abolished by a standing order.

The presence of legislators can only be dispensed with by leave of absence, or employment
in the service of the body. Absenteeism may
be carried so far as to obstruct business and
prevent a quorum, which result is very unjust
to members who attend faithfully to their public
duties, as well as unfair to the constituents of
the absentees. In Congress, the Constitution
itself authorizes less than a quorum to compel
the attendance of absentees; and the rules of
both Houses prohibit the absence of members
without leave first obtained. The law requires
salary to be deducted for absence of a Senator

or Representative, except in case of his illness or that of his family. The names of members absent on yea and nay votes are recorded, and published in the journals and in the *Congressional Record*.

In Parliament, urgent business or family affliction is regarded as ground for a leave of absence, although it is occasionally refused.

Bills.

In all legislative bodies, the questions most frequently pending are in the form of bills or of resolutions. A bill is any proposed act of legislation, and begins with the formula (in Congress): *"Be it enacted by the Senate and House of Representatives of the United States of America, in Congress assembled."* Before 1871, every section of a bill began with the words *"and be it further enacted;"* and the statute-books were thus encumbered with many pages of this tedious and useless verbiage. No enacting formula is now used in any section of a bill or law except the first. In the Senate, one day's notice must be given to introduce a new bill, unless by unanimous consent. In the House,

the Speaker must call the States and Territories
in the order of the alphabet on every Monday,
for bills offered by the members for printing and
reference, without debate. Of each bill 750
copies are printed, and reprints or extra copies
are often ordered. The number of bills offered
in Congress is enormously large, and annually
increasing, now exceeding 7,000 for a long session, and much beyond that for a Congress.
Bills are at once referred, by announcement of
the Speaker, to the committees to which, under
the rules, they properly belong by their subject-
matters. When committees have considered
any bills referred to them, they usually report
them back with a recommendation either: (1) if
adversely decided, that the committee be discharged from further consideration of the
bill, and that it be indefinitely postponed; (2)
if favorably reported, that the bill, with or without amendments of the committee, be placed
upon the calendar or (in some cases, by unanimous consent or suspension of the rules) put
upon its passage. In the House there are six
privileged committees having the right to report
bills or resolutions at any time, namely: the

Committee on Elections, as to the right of members to seats in the House; the Committee of Ways and Means, on revenue bills; the Committee of Appropriations, on general appropriation bills; the Committee on Printing, on matters relating thereto; the Committee on Accounts, on House expenditures; and the Committee on Enrolled Bills, such bills as are enrolled. Other bills from committees must take their chance of being reported back when the committee is called in its order. It is usual, when bills are first reported from committees, to have them printed and recommitted, which gives time for examination before they are called up for action. When a bill is taken up for consideration, the rule requires it to be read in full, if demanded by any member. It is customary, however, to read bills only by title, except upon their passage, when a full reading is mandatory. Every bill must be read three times: the first and second readings by title, the third reading in full when put upon its passage, or by sections when debated and amended. When a bill has been read three times, the Chair puts the question: "Shall the bill pass?" After this no amendment can be offered, but it is open to debate, unless the previous question on its passage has been demanded and seconded by the House. No bill can be amended by the addition of any other pending bill or its substance. There are various ways of defeating a bill, besides the direct one of rejection. These are: (1) To move to strike out the enacting words or clause of the bill. This has precedence of motions to amend, and, if carried, is equivalent to its rejection. (2) By moving to lay the bill on the table, which motion takes precedence of every other except to adjourn, and must be decided without debate. If a bill is laid on the table, it is considered as finally defeated, as it is very rarely taken up again during the session. (3) By a motion to commit or recommit the bill. This is a common method of defeating or indefinitely postponing a measure which a majority do not deem it expedient to defeat by a direct vote; it is often made the means to bury a bill in committee, when it is known to be almost certain that the committee will find no opportunity to report it back (even if favorably inclined) at the same session.

When any bill is passed, the committee chairman, or the member having it in charge, moves that the vote which passed it be reconsidered, and that the motion to reconsider be laid on the table. If this motion is carried, no reconsideration can take place, and the passage of the bill is settled. In the Senate, however, no formality of a reconsideration and of laying that motion on the table prevails in the passage of bills. The Senate rule requires each bill and resolution to receive three readings previous to its passage. These readings must be on three different days, unless the Senate unanimously direct otherwise (as is frequently done). Bills reported from Senate committees must go on the calendar in the order reported. House bills, if not referred to Senate committees, are placed on the calendar in their order, unless (as happens in rare cases) they are considered at once by unanimous consent. Bills introduced on leave, as well as House bills, may be read twice, if not objected to, for reference to committees, but cannot, on the same day, be reconsidered nor debated, if any objection is made. After a bill is read in the Senate a third time, amendments are not in order, except by unanimous consent; but it is in order at any time before the passage of any bill to move to commit it. Amendments to appropriation bills are not in order in the Senate if increasing appropriations, unless to carry out provisions of law previously passed, or unless moved by some committee. Any amendment proposed to a bill may be laid on the table without carrying with it or prejudicing the bill itself. All bills passed by either House must be certified by its clerical officer, and, with his signature and the date of their passage, are conveyed by him or an assistant Clerk to the other House. Bills passed in one House and rejected in the other, must be notified to the former. Such bills cannot be revived the same session except by a two-thirds vote, and after ten days' notice. While bills are on their passage between the two Houses, they are engrossed on paper; when passed by both branches, they are enrolled on parchment, and compared or collated by the Joint Committee on Enrolled Bills. After this they must be signed by the President of the Senate and the Speaker of the House, and presented by a member of the last-named committee to the President for his signature. This frequently involves some delay, as the Executive (sometimes with the aid of his constitutional advisers) has to examine all bills for approval or objections. When signed by the President, bills are permanently filed in the Department of State, where they form the official acts of Congress, from which the " Statutes at Large " are printed. The President's approval of any bill is communicated by message to the House in which the bill originated, and this is entered upon the journal. If a bill is not returned by the President within ten days, it becomes a law by the Constitution, unless Congress meanwhile adjourns, in which case it does not become a law. Bills from which the President withholds his signature are usually returned within the ten days with his objections, when it requires a vote of two-thirds of the members present in each House to make them laws, notwithstanding the President's objections.

Private Bills.

Private bills are defined to be those for the benefit of individuals, corporations, etc. Every

Friday in each week is devoted, by rule of the
House, to their consideration. Private bills,
when reported from committees, must be considered in Committee of the Whole. The Senate has a rule that, when any private bill is considered, it is in order, as a substitute for it, to
refer the case to the Court of Claims for hearing
and decision.

In the British Parliament, there prevails a
radical distinction between public and private
bills, which is not recognized in Congress. Private bills, for the interest of individuals, corporations or localities, must be brought before
the body by petition, and taken charge of by
a parliamentary agent. These agents are required to obey all the rules and practice of the
House of Commons, to be registered, and to
give bond in the sum of £500, to fix their responsibility. The time for considering private
bills in Parliament is immediately after the
meeting of the House. Private bills are, when
set down for hearing, distinguished into opposed
and unopposed bills. They are heard before
committees upon private bills, and an elaborate

method of procedure is laid down by standing orders. The chief responsibility rests with the chairman of the Ways and Means, who is charged with the special duty of examining, with the legal counsel of the Speaker, every private bill.

In Congress, the great variety and constantly increasing number of bills for the relief of private parties, engross altogether too much time of the body and of its committees. This is to the prejudice of the public business, which is more and more thrown into arrears, and has led to many propositions for relief, including the reference of all private bills to the Court of Claims, or to create some new tribunal to hear and adjudicate all claims against the government.

Bills containing appropriations of money may originate in either House of Congress, but all bills for raising revenue must, by constitutional requirement, originate in the House of Representatives, though the Senate's power of amendment is complete. In fact, that body has sometimes taken such liberties with revenue bills, in spite of the jealousy of the House of its prerogative in matters of revenue, as to make an entirely new measure out of a revenue bill sent to it from the House. The most recent and extreme instance of this was in the Tariff Revision act of 1883. In this case the Senate amended a little internal revenue reduction bill, passed by the House, by engrafting on it a thorough revision of the entire tariff system, and this, with some amendments, was accepted and passed by the House. In the Senate, the Committee on Finance has charge of all revenue bills. In the House, they belong to the Committee of Ways and Means. It is always in order, after the morning hour, to report or to move to consider appropriation bills, or bills respecting the tariff or internal revenue.

The term "Omnibus Bill" is sometimes applied in Congress to a bill embracing numerous distinct objects, as in the bill "making appropriations for sundry civil expenses of the government, and for other purposes."

The preamble to a bill or resolution (when it embodies a preamble) is, by general parliamentary usage, postponed until the main body of the bill or the substantive clauses of the resolution have been considered, after which the question is taken on agreeing to the preamble. A motion to strike out the preamble, or to amend it, may be made. When (as often happens) no separate vote on the preamble is demanded, the question may be taken on the whole, or the preamble may be considered as adopted *sub silentio*.

Revenue bills are known in Parliament as money bills, and must originate in the House of Commons. Amendments to them by the Lords must not change the intention of the Commons by increase or deduction, or manner of raising the revenue.

In the House of Lords, public bills may be offered without notice, but leave must be obtained in the Commons on notice previously given. Bills which have passed both Houses receive the royal assent by commission under the great seal. Occasionally the Queen assents to bills in person in the House of Lords.

In the French *Corps Législatif*, bills are proposed by the Ministry or by members of either Chamber, when they are printed and referred to the proper committees. Reports upon bills are

printed, after which the Chamber fixes a time
for discussion. No bill can become a law until
it has had two deliberations, with at least five
days interval between them, except financial
bills, and bills declared to be urgent.

Bribery.

Any attempt to bribe a member of a legislative body is a breach of the privileges of the
House. In Congress, several instances of lob-
byists and others, charged with bribery, appear
in the journals. The earliest case was that of
Robert Randall, in 1795, who combined with
Charles Whitney and others in forming a " ring "
to procure from Congress a grant of twenty
millions of acres of Western lands for a sum
merely nominal. In this case, one member
was offered money, and four were promised
shares in the land grant if they would lend
their aid to the scheme. Randall pretended
that they had secured a majority of the Senate
and thirty or forty Representatives, but on investigation admitted the utter falsity of the
statement. Even before the bill appropriating
the lands was offered, he was exposed through

members whom he had approached, arrested by the order of the House, brought to the bar and reprimanded by the Speaker, and discharged after two weeks' imprisonment. In the case of John Anderson, in 1818, the inculpated person offered a fee of five hundred dollars to the chairman of the House Committee on Claims, "for extra trouble in making a report." The offer was at once laid before the House by the member, and on his motion Anderson was arrested, imprisoned and publicly reprimanded at the bar of the House.

In the case of the Pacific Mail Steamship subsidy in 1872, which was passed, increasing the annual grant for carrying the mail from California to China and Japan from $500,000 to $1,000,000, the subsidy was repealed ten years later, when an investigation was had. The Committee of Ways and Means reported that no money was found to have been paid to any member of Congress, but the Pacific Mail Company had expended about $800,000 in employing lobbyists, journalists, and obscure employees of Congress, besides an ex-Congressman or two, for supposed influence in the

House or Senate. R. B. Irwin, the agent in
these heavy disbursements, was examined as a
witness, but obstinately refused to testify.

Bribery or corruption in the election of a
Senator has more than once been charged, but
the only case in which the Senate Committee
on Privileges and Elections have reported that
it existed, was in the resolution adopted March
4, 1873, that Alexander Caldwell, who had been
returned by the Legislature of Kansas, "was
not duly and legally elected a Senator," where-
upon he resigned his seat.

Call of the House.

The motion for a call of the House or Senate
is in order whenever no quorum is found to be
present. In the Senate, the rule requires the
Sergeant-at-Arms, when directed by a majority
of the Senators present, to request, and when
necessary to compel, the attendance of absent
Senators, when upon a call of the Senate it is
found without a quorum. After such a call,
and pending the execution of the order to sum-
mon absentees, no debate nor motion except to
adjourn is in order until a quorum appears. A

call of the House proceeds in the same manner, the names of absentees being noted by the Clerk, after which the doors are closed, and the Sergeant-at-Arms or his deputies sent to arrest absentees wherever found. When absent members are brought in, they are produced at the bar, and must render their excuses for absence to the Speaker, the House deciding upon what condition (of fine, etc.) they may be discharged from arrest. Calls of the House are most frequent during night sessions, and are sometimes the signal for great disorder and merriment over the excuses trumped up by the arrested members. No motion can be made during the call except to adjourn the House, or that all further proceedings under the call be dispensed with. Upon the appearance of a quorum, the latter motion is generally made.

Censure.

A motion to censure a member of a legislative body may be proposed when he has violated the rules in debate, or by disorderly conduct, or by any act is held to deserve the censure of the House. If the motion to censure prevails, the rule requires the Speaker to pronounce

(I)

that such a member (calling him by name at
the bar) has incurred the censure of the House.
Resolutions of censure have been frequently introduced in Congress, chiefly for transgressions
of the rules of debate by violent or insulting
remarks. Sometimes they have been withdrawn
after proper apology, and sometimes passed.
Instances have occurred also where the Speaker
has been required to pronounce the censure of
the House upon members guilty of grave der-
elictions in their capacity of Representatives ([1]).

(1.) Joshua R.Giddings, of Ohio, was censured by vote of the House
March 22, 1842, for presenting resolutions denouncing the domestic
traffic in slaves. He at once resigned his seat, but was returned by
a great majority Resolutions of censure and expulsion were introduced in July, 185^, against Preston S. Brooks, of S. C., for a violent assault upon Charles Sumner in the Senate Chamber, but failed
to pass, although commanding a majority (a two-thirds vote being
required to expel). Mr. Brooks resigned, but was immediately re-
elected. In the same case, July 15, 1856, the Houe " declared its
disapprobation " of the action of Lawrenc: M. Keitt, of S. C., in aid-
ing and abetting the assault. Mr. Keitt resigned his seat, but was returned at the same session. April 14, 1864, Alexander Long, of Ohio,
was declared by vote of a majority "an unworthy member of the
House" for certain utterances regarding the war for the Union. Feb.
28, 1870, the House passed resolutions of censure upon J. T. Deweese,
of N. C., who had sold an appointment to a West Point Cadetship,
a previously offered resolution of expulsion being withdrawn because
of his resignation before the vote was taken. March 3, 1873, a resolution declaring that "the House absolutely condemns the conduct "
of Oakes Ames and of James Brooks, in the Credit Mobilier matter,
was passed.

Others than Representatives, also, have been publicly reprimanded at the bar of the House by the Speaker for various offenses.

The Speaker of the House of Commons has been many times directed by the House to reprimand or admonish at the bar persons who have offended against the dignity of the body.

In the French Chamber, censure, with forfeiture of salary, may be passed upon members refusing to heed a call to order, or raising a tumult, or menacing or insulting any member. In case of resistance by any deputy, or of tumult in the Chamber, the rule requires the President to adjourn the session at once.

Clôture.

The meaning of this term, recently adopted from the French into parliamentary law, is the closing of debate. It corresponds closely to the previous question, as it prevails in American assemblies. Up to 1882, there was no standing order in the British House of Commons which enabled a majority of the House to control its business by closing debate, and thus secure the passage of measures brought in by the Ministry in power by the will of the House. At two successive sessions of Parliament in 1881–2, there occurred a bitter and protracted struggle between the majority and a small minority of Home Rulers, chiefly Irish members, over the proposed legislation investing the government with power to enforce the laws in Ireland. About forty members successfully struggled for months against an overwhelming majority, by taking advantage of the rules of the House, which were designed to promote freedom of discussion. Scenes of great disorder, with many all-night sessions of the House, resulted from these obstructive tactics. The Home Rule members continually renewed their motions to adjourn the debate, to adjourn the House, etc., striving to weary out the majority, and defeat or postpone the obnoxious Irish bill. The Liberal majority, aided on this occasion by the Conservative party, who made common cause with the followers of Gladstone, kept the House together by relays of members relieving each other, and the debate went on day and night. At length, by a decisive assumption of power on the part of the Speaker in putting the question to vote, the debate was arrested, and the Irish members left the House in a body. Upon the Irish bill reaching a second reading, the same obstructions were renewed, and the Speaker called by name Mr. Parnell, and other members who had disregarded the authority of the Chair, and violated the rules of the House. A motion to expel for the day thirty-one of the Home Rule party was carried through; and soon after, the Gladstone resolution declaring the " urgency " of the bill was carried, 359 to 56. This secured parliamentary progress, and the Irish bill was passed through both Houses. At the next session of Parliament, in 1882, the Ministerial resolutions adopting new rules of procedure as a permanent standing order, in which the *clôture* was the leading feature, were carried after months of contest and debate. These new parliamentary rules are to the following effect: 1, provides that the Speaker or Chairman may stop the debate at his discretion, if supported by more than 200 members, or if opposed by less than 40 and supported by more than 100; 2, provides that motions for adjournment for the discussion of a definite matter of urgent importance, shall be entertained if 40 members support it by rising up ; 3, provides for limiting such debate to the subject in hand ; 4, provides for the taking of divisions ; 5, 6 and 7, are technical rules for the Speaker's or Chairman's guidance; 8, makes it a standing order that no opposed motion shall be taken after half-past 12 at night ; 9, regulates the suspension of offending members; 10, gives the Speaker or Chairman the power to check attempts to secure delay by abuse of the rules ; 11 and 12, are minor provisions ; and 13, makes the first seven and last three resolutions into standing orders.

By the *règlement* of the French Chamber of Deputies, the President cannot pronounce the *clôture* to stop debate until he has taken the sense of the Chamber. In case the *clôture* is opposed, only one speech against it is permitted. When the *clôture* is once pronounced, no further debate is in order except brief remarks upon the state of the question.

Consent.

A motion for unanimous consent is made to make some business in order which would be out of order under the rules. In the ordinary course of business at public meetings, as well as in parliamentary bodies, any matter may receive consideration by unanimous consent. In the Senate often, and sometimes in the House, legislation goes forward when it is well known that no quorum is present to legislate, simply because no member objects. The method of proceeding in any assembly is for a member to address the Chair : " I ask unanimous consent to offer, or to take up," etc. The presiding officer then says : " Is it the pleasure of the assembly that " (such a thing should be done)? If no member rises to dissent, he announces : " The Chair hears no objection," and the matter is ordered, without putting the question in any other shape. If any member objects, there is of course an end to the motion for unanimous consent, and the rules as to the order of business must be adhered to. The introduction of any bill or resolution out of its regular order requires unanimous consent. The most frequent requests for unanimous consent are to have leave to print remarks which members were prevented from making in open House ; to be excused from the House, or from voting; to have time extended when speaking; to withdraw papers from the files; to take up a bill or motion for present consideration, etc. If no objection is heard, the Chair announces that the request is granted.

As no business in the House can be taken up out of regular order without consent of all, the right to object becomes very important, as a single member may thus defeat or postpone a measure, unless two-thirds of the House agree to suspend the rules.

Elections.

The election of members of Congress is a question of the highest privilege, the Constitution itself making each House the judge of the elections, returns and qualifications of its own members. The Committee on Elections stands at the head of the list of committees in each House. Contested elections of members, of which several are found in every Congress, are carefully examined by these committees. The law requires any contestant of the election of a Representative to notify the member claiming to be elected of his proposal to contest the seat, within thirty days after the result is declared. The member being required to answer within thirty days, each side is allowed ninety days longer to take testimony. The written testimony is sent to the Clerk of the House, and usually printed. Persons contesting the seats of members have the privilege of the floor pending the decision of their claim, and can be heard in their own behalf before a vote is taken. Questions of the right of a member to his seat take precedence of all other business. It is usual to vote an unsuccessful contestant, or a sitting member who is displaced by a contestant whose claim is favorably reported, a handsome sum (now limited by statute to $2,000) for the expenses of making the contest.

The election of Representatives in Congress is fixed by act of March 3, 1875, to be held on a uniform day in all the States, viz., on the Tuesday next after the first Monday in November, every second year, in 1876, and following even years. But States whose constitutions fix a different election-day may elect earlier, until they amend their constitutions. Of these, only Ohio, West Virginia and Iowa remain.

The election of Senators must, by law of Congress, be made by the Legislature chosen next before the expiration of the term of a Senator. Each House must proceed to ballot for a Senator on the second Tuesday after its organization, and at least one ballot must be taken daily until a choice is effected. Both Houses meet in joint assembly after the first separate vote, and a majority of this assembly is required to elect.

In the British Parliament, where the trial of contests for seats by the House of Commons had led to great abuses by partisan majorities, the entire jurisdiction in the trial of controverted elections was transferred in 1868 to the courts of law.

Expulsion.

The motion to expel a member from either House of Congress requires a vote of two-thirds, under a provision of the Constitution itself. This high power has been several times exercised, although more frequently it has happened that resolutions of expulsion have been lost through not commanding a two-thirds vote. They have also frequently been forestalled by the resignation of the offending member. In the Senate, July 8, 1797, William Blount, of Tennessee, was expelled for instigating Indians to aid the British arms in West Florida. A similar resolution to expel John Smith, a Senator from Ohio, for complicity in Aaron Burr's treasonable movement in 1806, was lost by one vote, and the Senator afterward resigned. On the 5th of February, 1862, Jesse .D. Bright, a Senator from Indiana, was expelled for alleged disloyalty to the government, by a vote of 32 to 14. In the case of O. B. Matteson, W. A. Gilbert, and other members in 1853, the House of Representatives being about to vote on resolutions of expulsion of the inculpated members for corruption in railway land grants, the resignations of the members were tendered on the same day the expulsion resolutions were before the House. In the case of B. F. Whittemore, of South Carolina, whom a committee of the House, in 1870, reported guilty of selling an appointment to a cadetship at West Point Military Academy, resolutions of expulsion were brought in, but the member resigned his seat an hour or two before the question was to be taken. The resolutions were then laid on the table. Whittemore was, however, re-elected to the same House, but that body passed a resolution returning to him his credentials, and refusing to allow him to be sworn in as a member. The same year, J. T. Deweese, a Representative from North Carolina, having confessed to a committee of investigation that he had received $500 on account of an appointment to West Point, was about to be expelled, but resigned his seat before the vote was taken.

In the British House of Commons, a considerable number of cases of expulsion have occurred for such grave offenses as corruption, perjury, conspiracy, fraud, libel, forgery, etc. The latest instance of expulsion was that of James Sadleir, in 1857, for fraud.

Expunging.

Legislative bodies have sometimes rescinded the action of a former legislative body, by passing a resolution to expunge from the journals some action or resolution formerly adopted. This is a very questionable procedure, since it undertakes to mutilate a record, or to falsify the actual proceedings of the body. The most remarkable instance in Congress (and the only case found) was the passage of the famous expunging resolution offered by Senator Thomas H. Benton in 1837, to erase from the journal the resolution passed by the Senate of 1834 censuring President Jackson for assuming "powers not conferred by the Constitution and laws, but in derogation of both."

In the House of Commons, entries in the journal have sometimes been expunged by vote of the House. In 1782, the House reversed the action of its predecessors in the case of John Wilkes, who had been repeatedly expelled from Parliament, and ordered this vote expunged from the journals, as "subversive of the rights of the whole body of electors of this kingdom."

Filibustering.

This significant term, used in a parliamentary sense, is applied to the motions, oft-repeated and renewed, for dilatory and obstructive purposes, by the minority. In the House of Representatives, nearly every session for years has witnessed what are termed filibustering tactics, to defeat or to postpone action upon an obnoxious measure. The minority insist upon the right to call the yeas and nays on every question. Then, by constantly renewing motions to adjourn, to adjourn to a fixed day, to reconsider, etc., and by successive relays of members to raise questions of order and parliamentary inquiries, long sessions are consumed, sometimes lasting all night, in the endeavor to weary out the majority, or to compel them to some compromise. The latter end is frequently reached, and the determination of one party is broken by the determined resistance of the other. In the Senate, where there is little check upon debate (and some notable filibustering contests have come in the House from denial of full discussion by the majority), a milder kind of filibustering is sometimes carried on by a well-organized minority occupying the floor in succession, and each speaking as long as possible to prevent a vote. Measures are some-

times defeated by these tactics consuming the
entire time of a session about to close.

Order.

The order of the day in an assembly or legislative body is the regular routine fixed by the
rules for the consideration of business. To call
for the "regular order" is to demand of the presiding officer that the body be recalled from
other matters, or from what may be proposed
by certain members out of due order, and proceed to the unfinished business, or to whatever
is prescribed by the rules.

Special orders are subjects fixed in advance
for a particular day, requiring a two-thirds vote
for their assignment, though they may be postponed by a majority vote when their time
arrives.

To preserve order in the assembly is the
first duty of the presiding officer. Either the
Chair or any member of the body may call to
order members transgressing the rules. When
the call to order is made, the member on the
floor, though in the midst of a sentence, must
sit down at once, unless permitted to explain by

unanimous consent. If called to order for words spoken in debate, they must be reduced to writing and read to the House. The House must, if appealed to, decide on the case without debate ; if the decision is in favor of the member called to order, he is at liberty to proceed, but not otherwise.

When a point of order of any kind is made, it is the duty of the Chair to decide it forthwith (1). This he may do by sustaining the point of order as well taken, or by overruling it ; and the business moves on in accordance with his decision, unless appealed from. Questions of order do not require to be seconded, but may be raised by any member, and at any time except when a division is going on.

Petitions.

The former usage in Congress was that members presented petitions in open House, but this led to so great a waste of time (many hundred

---

(1) The exception is when the presiding officer is not required (as he is by the House rules) to determine points of order, but may submit them to the assembly at his option, to be determined. Thus, the Senate rule permits the presiding officer to decide, or to refer to the decision of the Senate, any question of order.

petitions and memorials being sometimes offered in a day), that the rule was changed. Members now deliver at the Clerk's desk the petitions they are requested to offer, endorsing them with their names, and the specific committee reference desired. In the Senate, they continue to be presented publicly during the morning hour.

In Parliament, all petitions (which are presented in great numbers) must have original signatures. They are referred by the rules, without debate, to the Committee on Public Petitions.

The French Chambers order a brief of petitions printed for the use of members. A Committee on Petitions classifies them, referring some to government officers and others to the consideration of the Chamber. Each petitioner is advised of the disposition made. Twice a year the Ministers distribute a printed report to the members, stating what action they have taken upon petitions referred to them.

Previous Question. (See Cloture, p. 107.)

This important motion puts it in the power of a majority to close debate at any time by ordering the vote immediately on the question

under consideration. It is not in order to debate
nor to amend the motion for the previous question. It yields only to questions of order or
of privilege, or to the motion to lay on the table.
When any member of the assembly calls for the
previous question, if there is a second, the presiding officer must immediately inquire : " Shall
the main question be now put ? " If a majority
vote in the affirmative and the previous question
is ordered, the member who offered or reported
from a committee the matter before the House
is entitled to the floor to close the debate (this
being the only exception to the peremptory cut-
ting off of discussion). After this the Chair
puts the questions before the assembly in their
order of precedence, until the main question,
with all subsidiary ones, is disposed of. The previous question was first recognized in Congress
in the earliest rules of the House in 1789, which
directed that it might be demanded by five
members. It does not prevail in the Senate,
where debate is without limit, unless rules are
agreed upon to limit it (as in Committee of the
Whole).

If the motion for the previous question fails

to command a majority, the discussion continues just as if the motion had not been made.
The call may be limited to ordering the previous
question on an amendment, and when this is
disposed of the main question will be again
open to debate, unless the mover has taken the
precaution to include in his call the pending
question and all amendments thereto. It is
held by some that a two-thirds vote should be
required for the adoption of any motion to cut
off debate; but in the absence of any rule in the
constitution or by-laws of the body, the requirement of a simple majority (as in the House of
Representatives) is prevalent, and is more in
consonance with that progress which is so important in the business of associations of any
kind.

There are various methods to prevent the
consideration of any question which it is desired by any portion of the assembly to suppress.
One of these is for a member to object to the
consideration of the question at the outset, and
before discussion. This raises the question of
consideration (not requiring a second), and the
Chair must inquire: " Will the assembly con-

sider this question?" If the vote is in the negative, the question is at once removed from before the body, and cannot be brought up again during the same sitting.

The most usual motion to defeat the consideration of a question after debate, is to move that it be indefinitely postponed. This can only be made when no other motion is pending except a main question, and it is open to debate, unlike the motion for the previous question. It yields only to a preferred question, and is not amendable. If carried, it removes the main question from consideration during the sitting.

Another and most effective method of getting rid of a question without action, is to move to lay it upon the table. This motion is not debatable nor subject to amendment, and if carried by a majority, it removes the question from consideration. But being simply laid upon the table until the assembly wish to consider it, this disposition is not final (unless there is a rule making it so), but simply avoids the question while there is a majority opposed to its consideration. It is an ancient rule of Parliament that "a question being once made, and carried in the affirmative or negative, cannot be questioned again, but must stand as a judgment of the House." The *rationale* of this rule is that it is necessary, to save the time of the body from being wasted in the discussion of motions of the same nature. Contradictory decisions would often be arrived at during the same session, and it is obvious that some things must be accepted as settled. But in practice there is much latitude, even in Parliament, and successful evasions of the rule occur by members changing the character of the motion sufficiently to constitute a new question.

Privilege.

A distinction is to be drawn between a privileged question and a question of privilege. The latter involves the character and prerogatives of the assembly or its members, and will here be treated first; the former respects the order of precedence accorded to the various matters coming before an assembly.

A question of privilege, if actually decided by the presiding officer to be such, takes precedence of any business in hand, because it concerns the rights of the assembly or of its members. It may relate to disturbances of the proceedings, to menace or insult of a member, to attacks upon character in a representative capacity, etc. A question of privilege may be debated, postponed to a time fixed, referred to a committee for inquiry and report, or laid on the table. The Chair must promptly decide, when first proposed, whether the matter brought forward presents a question of privilege or not; from this decision an appeal lies to the assembly.

When any question raised by a member presents a question of privilege, in the judgment of the presiding officer, he must entertain it in preference to all other business; but the too common practice of members undertaking to make personal explanations under the plea of a privileged question, should not be tolerated in any well-officered deliberative or legislative body. The plain reason is that one member has no right to consume the time of all the rest, and ob-struct the public business, to listen to his personal grievances. If one member, for example, may bring the shield of the rules to cover his personal defense against newspaper attacks, all the members may insist upon the same right—a result which would be obviously intolerable. The rule of the House of Representatives is, that questions of privilege affecting members individually must relate to their representative capacity only. -It has now become the well-settled practice, when a member rises to a question of privilege based upon a newspaper publication, for the Speaker to hold that such publication must assail or reflect upon the member in his official capacity; that is, connect him with alleged corrupt or improper influences as to some matter of legislation; otherwise it is not a matter of privilege.

In the House of Representatives, the highest privilege attaches to questions affecting the rights of the House itself, maintaining its dignity, and the integrity of its proceedings. The privilege of a Representative rests upon the right of his constituency to be always represented in his person. The Constitution itself provides that Senators and Representatives shall not be questioned elsewhere for any speech or debate in either House, and shall be privileged from arrest during the sessions, and in going and returning. In maintaining their privileges, both Houses of Congress have repeatedly directed reporters to be excluded from the hall, or ordered the Speaker to reprimand an offending person at the bar of the House, or directed the arrest of the accused, or committed them to custody within the Capitol, or ordered a refractory witness or a person assaulting a member, to be imprisoned in the jail of the District of Columbia. The most frequent cases in which Congress asserts its privilege are the refusals of witnesses to testify before its committees. Many recusant witnesses have been imprisoned until the expiration of the Congress, or until they have repented and agreed to answer, or until discharged from custody by vote of the majority. The stretch of power by which a legislative body exercises the functions of a court has always been controverted. While it cannot be denied that the power, if it exists, is extra-constitutional, it is asserted, on the other hand, that the power to compel testimony relating to matters of public legislation is inherent in every legislative body, has been frequently exercised by Congress and by State Legislatures, and is essential to their power and proper functions. The power is limited by some State constitutions, which prohibit any imprisonment by legislative authority beyond a certain term of hours or days. While in some early cases this power in Congress has been maintained by the Supreme Court, on the basis of right and necessity, the Court held, in Kilbourn *v.* Thompson, in 1880, that imprisonment for refusal to divulge to a committee of Congress the private accounts of a company in a matter under investigation by the House, was illegal and unconstitutional. Kilbourn had been imprisoned forty-five days in jail as a recusant witness, and the Speaker who signed the warrant, the Sergeant-at-Arms who held the prisoner in custody, and the committee who brought in the resolution for imprisonment, were joined as defendants in a suit for damages brought by Kilbourn. In the case of the members of the House, the Court held their constitutional privilege to be a good defense, but the order of the House declaring the witness guilty of contempt of its authority, and ordering his imprisonment, was adjudged void, and as affording the Sergeant-at-Arms no pro-

tection in the suit brought by the witness. The
Constitution gave the House no power to pun-
ish for contempt, and no authority to compel a
witness to testify where the subject-matter of
the investigation was judicial and not legislative (103 U. S. Reports, 168). In this case,
after the above adjudication, three several trials
were had in the Court below, involving the
measure of damages to be awarded plaintiff as
against the Sergeant-at-Arms. The first jury
awarded him $100,000; but this and the award
of a second ($60,000) and a third jury ($37,-
500) were all set aside as excessive, the Court
finally permitting the defendant to recover $20,-
000 damages.

Many questions of privilege, growing out of the refusal of witnesses to testify, have arisen in Congress.   John Nugent, a New
York *Herald* correspondent, who procured from a Senator the Guada-
loupe-Hidalgo treaty with Mexico in 1848, and published it, while
it was yet under injunction of secrecy and unratified in the Senate,
was examined by a committee as to the means by which he got the
treaty, and refusing to testify, was imprisoned six weeks by order of
the Senate.   In 1857, J. W. Simonton, of the New York *Times*,
was imprisoned January 21st, and kept in confinement nearly three
weeks by the House of Representatives, for refusing to divulge the
names of members who, as he had declared, were influenced by a
corrupt consideration in the railroad land grant legislation of that
year.   In 1868, C. W. Woolley was incarcerated from May 28th to
June 11th for refusing to testify regarding alleged corrupt transactions in securing the acquittal of President Johnson in the im-

In the British Parliament, many arbitrary acts of tyranny have been visited upon persons held guilty of violating the privileges of that body. But though maintained by the Court of King's Bench, the right to imprison a subject for contempt of the House has long been regarded with increasing jealousy.

The following list, made up from the journals, summarizes the more important questions

---

peachment proceedings before the Senate. In 1871, Z. L. White and H. J. Ramsdell, newspaper correspondents, were held in confinement, by order of the Senate, for nine days, because they refused to divulge how they obtained the Treaty of Washington (Alabama Claims) for publication, before it was ratified by the Senate. In 1870, one Patrick Woods, for an assault upon Charles H. Porter, a member of the House, in the streets of Richmond, Va., was brought to Washington and confined in the district jail for three months, by order of the House. In February, 1873, J. B. Stewart, an attorney, was imprisoned in the Capitol some thirty days, as a recusant witness in the Credit Mobilier investigation. In January, 1875, R. B. Irwin was kept in close custody more than two weeks for refusing to reveal the names of corrupt parties who had profited by the Pacific Mail Steamship subsidy ring.

In January, 1877, Enos Runyon was imprisoned for refusing to testify regarding certain transactions as to the Electoral vote of Oregon.

In March, 1800, William Duane, editor of the Philadelphia *Aurora*, was arrested by order of the Senate, and brought to its bar for alleged defamatory publications concerning Senators. Motions were made to imprison him, and to prosecute him under the Sedition law, but the matter was dropped without action. March 4th, 1846, the reporters of the New York *Tribune* were expelled from the House of Representatives on account of correspondence ridiculing William Sawyer, a Representative from Ohio.

which have been adjudged matters of privilege in Congress: Assault upon a member; duel between two members, or challenge of a member; disorder in the gallery; offer to bribe a member; refusal of witnesses to appear before committees, or refusal to testify; right of a member to· be seated; election of a Speaker; menacing language toward a member; refusal of a member to take his seat when ordered by the Chair; violent language toward members in debate; fracas between two reporters in presence of the House; a motion to impeach the President; alleged mutilation of the journal; charges affecting official character of a member; protest by the President against proceedings of the House; misconduct of the House printer in publishing charges in his newspaper; alleged false report of House proceedings by one of its reporters; alteration and interpolation in House bills; misconduct of an officer of the House; divulging the secrets of the body; alleged corrupt combinations by members.

Privileged questions, specifically made such by the rules, are of different grades. Motions to adjourn, to fix the day to which the House shall adjourn, and to take a recess, are privileged, because always in order. Motions to reconsider stand next in privilege (in the House of Representatives), taking precedence of all other questions except those of adjournment and the consideration of conference reports. The motion for a call of the House is privileged; so are resolutions of inquiry directed to the heads of executive departments, when reported from committees (except on Friday). Reports from the six committees who have leave to report at any time, are privileged questions. A motion to consider a bill returned with the Presidential veto, is a privileged question under the Constitution. The previous question applies upon questions of privilege, as well as in other cases.

Question.

Putting the question with propriety is one of the most important duties of a presiding officer; it is also one of the most frequent. Questions are to be put in the first instance in this form: "As many as are in favor (of the motion, resolution, bill, order, etc.) will say Aye." And

after the affirmative vote is heard, the Chair will
say: "As many as are opposed, will say No."
The Chair then decides according to the vol-
ume of voices on each side, and announces,
"The Ayes have it," or "The Noes have it by
the sound," as the case may be. Other
methods of taking the question are considered
under VOTES. It is the duty of the Chair, before calling for the vote, to state the question
clearly to the assembly, being careful that the
body is in order at the time, that all may hear.
Mistakes in voting, both *viva voce*, and by all
other methods, are very common; they arise
frequently from want of precision and clearness
in stating the question by the Chair, as well as
through the inattention or preoccupation of
members, and from conversation and confusion
in the hall. It is, at every stage of the proceedings, the duty of the Chair to state the question
before the assembly, on request of any member.
A practice prevails in many assemblies, and
even in legislative bodies, for members to call
out "Question! Question!" or "Vote! Vote!"
when anxious for the progress of business, or
impatient of debate. Although this may be

technically a violation of the rules of order, yet as it tends to forward the matter in hand, and to bring tedious speakers to abridge their efforts, it should not be interfered with by a judicious presiding officer.

Any member of an assembly may ask a question of the Chair, but such inquiries should be confined to seeking information as to the question before the assembly, the effect of a certain motion, or vote, etc.; in short, such a question as will tend to elucidate the matter under consideration. In all formally organized or deliberative bodies, such questions should be introduced with the formula: " I rise to a parliamentary inquiry. Will the Chair state," etc.

In the British Parliament, questions are frequently put to the Ministry, or to a member of the Cabinet on the floor. One day's notice must be given of such questions by the members proposing to ask them. These questions must concern public measures or events, and while inquiry may be made as to the intentions of the government on any particular matter, they can not be questioned as to their opinions upon general matters of policy.

Recess.

A motion to take a recess, like that to adjourn, is privileged, and is not debatable. A recess is a qualified form of adjournment. To take a recess to a definite hour, whether of the same day or the day following, serves, in protracted sessions, when business presses, to give needful rest and refreshment to the members of the body, without long cessation of their public duties. In case of a recess, the legislative day runs on until an adjournment is had, and the journal bears the continuous date of that day.

The term Recess is also used to designate the interval between two annual or occasional sessions of Congress, usually continuing each year from the adjournment to the first Monday in December. Leave is frequently granted to committees in either House of Congress to sit during the recess in order to take testimony, to visit some part of the country upon the business of an investigation, or to mature business to be submitted to the respective Houses.

Reconsideration.

The motion to reconsider is of great importance, since, if it prevails, an action of the body
already taken is liable to be reversed. The only
method of bringing up, during the same sitting
of an assembly, a question once settled, is by a
motion to reconsider the vote on that question.
It is a privileged motion, taking precedence of
every other except those connected with adjournment. The motion to reconsider a question can be made only by a member who voted
with the majority when the question was
settled, unless there was no division of the
assembly thereon. The general rule is that the
motion must be made on the same day when
the vote was taken which it is sought to reconsider. In the Senate, however, it may be made
on the same day or on either of the next two
days of actual session; while in the House, it
must be made on the same day or the day following. The motion to reconsider a vote opens
up the original question to debate (except in the
Senate), in case that was a debatable question.
The motion may, however, be made and entered
(5)

on the minutes without immediate action, to be
called up at the next meeting, although this is a
matter to be settled by the rules of the body.
When the motion to reconsider is lost, it dis-
poses of the main question, which cannot again
be considered at the same sitting, unless a second motion to reconsider the vote by which the
assembly refuse to reconsider, should be made
and carried. When a motion to reconsider is
carried (which requires a majority only), the
presiding officer must state that the question
now recurs on the adoption of the main question, the vote on which is under reconsideration. This brings the original question before
the assembly in the same position as when it
was first voted upon, and it is treated in every
respect as an original question.

The motion to reconsider yields to privileged
questions only. In the Senate, the motion to
reconsider must be decided without debate, and
may be laid on the table, which, if carried, oper-
ates as a final disposition of the motion. If
the Senate desires to reconsider any bill, etc.,
which it has passed and sent to the House of
Representatives, the motion to reconsider must

be accompanied by a motion to request the House to return the same. If the motion to reconsider be lost, it can only be renewed by unanimous consent.

In the House, the motion to reconsider can be made only by a member who voted with the prevailing side, if the yeas and nays were taken; otherwise, any member may move a reconsideration. A motion to reconsider may be made regarding every question except to adjourn and to suspend the rules. It is debatable only when the question to be reconsidered was debatable, in which case it brings up for discussion the entire subject. The House has an important rule providing that no bill, resolution, etc., referred to a committee shall be brought back into the House on a motion to reconsider. Where a motion to reconsider has been once put and decided, it is not in order to repeat the motion, unless an amendment has been adopted since the first reconsideration, thus presenting new matter. A motion to reconsider a vote by which the House refused to adjourn is not in order, nor is a motion to reconsider a vote on the reconsideration of a vetoed bill; nor can a vote on a motion to suspend the rules be reconsidered. One kind of reconsideration which seems peculiar to the House of Representatives, is for the member having charge of a measure, as soon as the vote is taken upon it, to move to reconsider the vote last taken, and, also, to move that the motion to reconsider be laid on the table. If the latter motion prevails, it is deemed a finality so far as the vote proposed to be reconsidered is concerned.

In both houses of Parliament, a vote once taken cannot be reconsidered.

Reports.

In every deliberative body, reports form one of the most important classes of business coming before the assembly. The object of a report is, or should be, to present to the body a recommendation of some kind for its action, together with a statement of the reasons for that recommendation. Reports should be clearly and succinctly written, dealing only with the most important points of the case in hand, dwelling little, if at all, upon objections thereto, and avoiding all matters not immediately relevant to the question. The matter reported upon will thus be simplified for the action of the assembly, which can act understandingly only upon a clearly reasoned statement of each matter coming before it. All reports to an assembly come from committees, unless they are formal reports from its officers, and, as a rule, are required to be in writing. If the committee cannot agree on a unanimous report, it is in order for those dissenting to submit a minority report; and this should be read to the assembly with the report of the committee, as that agreed to by the majority is always termed. (*See* COMMITTEES, p. 53.)

In both Houses of Congress, it is usual to order reports to be printed and recommitted to the committee reporting them, or placed upon the calendar for future action. But it is not unusual, in the case of private bills or measures of pressing moment, to act upon them with merely a written report or recommendation of some committee.

In the Senate, reports of committees are called for and offered every morning, and must be printed, unless, for the dispatch of the business of the Senate, the printing is directed to be dispensed with. Reports of Senate committees must lie over one day for consideration, unless the Senate, by unanimous consent, directs otherwise.

The rules of the House provide for calling for the reports of committees daily in the morning hour, except on the first and third Mondays of each month. The reports which may be made from six committees are always in order; others must wait their day of unanimous consent, or a two-thirds majority to suspend the rules for their consideration.

Reports of Executive Departments are addressed to the Speaker of the House, or to the President of the Senate, and are always ordered to be printed and referred. It is the custom in the House for the Speaker, by unanimous consent, to lay such communications before the House, just after the approval of the journal, or the expiration of the morning hour, for reference. Such communications, and messages from the President, are the first business in order whenever the House proceeds to the consideration of business on the Speaker's table.

Each session's reports of the Senate and House committees make several bulky printed volumes, and the executive reports, both regular and special, fill a great many more.

In Parliament, reports from special committees or commissions are always published in folio as "blue books," with the evidence taken upon the subject-matters of the report, which is carefully indexed.

In the French Chambers, reports of committees must be printed at least twenty-four hours before the bill to which they relate is considered.

Reporters.

In all public assemblies, the importance of full public information causes special provision to be made for the reporters of the press. The Senate and the House of Representatives each employs a corps of five official short-hand reporters to write down the votes, proceedings and debates *verbatim*, for publication in the *Congressional Record* (styled the *Congressional Globe* until 1873), the next day. In the House, two reporters of the Associated Press are also admitted on the floor, while an ample reporters' gallery, directly over the Chair in both Houses, accommodates the representatives of the general press, under regulations made by the presiding officer.

The ancient usage in Parliament was to exclude all strangers, reporters included, on the motion of any member, and it was long made illegal to publish any of the proceedings or debates in Parliament. This was held to be a breach of the privileges of members of Parliament. Of late years the free admission of reporters is the rule, although exceptions are occasionally enforced on motion of members, reporters having been actually excluded as recently as in 1870 and 1878 to avoid publicity being given to debates.

In the French *Corps Législatif*, reporters are freely admitted to the galleries.

Resignations.

The resignation of a member of a deliberative body or of any society is considered as a right, while it sometimes presents a question of privilege. Vacancies caused by resignation, whether in the body itself or in its committees, are to be filled by the electing or appointing power, under such rules as are adopted. In Congress, the resignation of a Senator or Representative has always been treated in practice as an inherent right. It was never contested until the 41st Congress, when the Speaker decided that the member had the right to resign, and an appeal from the decision was laid upon the table by the House, thereby affirming it. When a Senator or Representative resigns his seat, his letter of resignation is addressed to the Governor of the State he represents, and, at the same time, it is the practice for a member resigning to notify the presiding officer of the body to which he belongs, in writing, of the action he has taken. In either case, there can be no acceptance or refusal to accept the resignation. Representatives resigning their seats in Congress, not infrequently address a public letter through the press to the people of the district which they represent, assigning reasons for the step taken.

Vacancies occurring in the Senate, whether by death or resignation (a case of long illness or other disability is not provided for), are notified to the Governor of the State, who may fill the vacancy by a Senator of his own appointment when the Legislature is not in session, pending the election of a Senator by the Legislature when next convened. A vacancy in the House of Representatives can be filled only by a new election by the people of the Congressional district which is left unrepresented, the day for such election being fixed by proclamation of the Governor of the State.

In Great Britain, it is a professedly settled principle of the law of Parliament that a member cannot relinquish his seat during the term for which he was elected. By an ingenious evasion of this restriction, however, a member wishing to resign asks to be appointed " Steward of the Chiltern Hundreds," an old and nominal office without any functions, which is given to any member who applies for it. Any acceptance of office under the Crown (except in the Ministry) legally vacating the seat of a member of Parliament, this obliges the House to order a new election.

Vacancies in the House of Commons are

filled by a new election held pursuant to a writ issued out of Chancery by a warrant from the Speaker.

In the French Chambers, any member has the right of resignation at any time.

Resolutions.

A resolution of an assembly is an expression of its opinion with regard to any matter, or a declaration of the purpose of the assembly. Resolutions in a society or permanent body are moved to accomplish many different objects: as to raise or to appropriate money, to impose a special tax upon the members, to authorize a member or a committee to perform some action, etc. All resolutions should be expressed in brief and clear terms, and should include one independent proposition, unless two entirely congruous ones can be united in one resolution to expedite business. It is quite usual for resolutions to be offered embracing incongruous and even contradictory matter. In such cases a division of the question should be called for before putting the resolution to vote. When a division of the question is ordered on a resolution, the first part is to be taken first, unless, for obvious reasons, the nature of the matters embraced indicates another order.

In Congress, frequent resolutions of inquiry are passed by either House, requesting certain information from the executive or the heads of departments. A resolution of one body, whether declaring the sense of the House or otherwise, does not bind Congress, and is not published in the statutes, but only in the journal of the House which passes it, and in the *Congressional Record*. A joint resolution, however, when passed by both Senate and House, has all the force of law. Such resolutions sometimes contain appropriations of public money. Resolutions conveying the thanks of Congress to military, naval or civil officers for distinguished public services, are always joint resolutions. Concurrent resolutions, unlike joint ones, do not require the signature of the President, and are not published in the statutes at large. They are passed to provide for the printing of documents, etc. The form of a concurrent resolution is as follows: "*Resolved*, by the Senate (the House of Representatives

concurring)," or *vice versa*. In the Senate, all
resolutions objected to must lie over one day.
In the House, it is customary to adopt, by resolution, the standing rules and orders for the
government of that body. It declares, by resolution, that it entertains certain opinions regarding public affairs, proposed legislation, or some
specific acts of government officials.

In the British Parliament, every resolution
reported by a committee may be amended, dis-
agreed to, postponed or recommitted.

Riders.

This term is applied to designate an amendment to a bill, tacking on to it, by a motion or
the action of a committee, subjects of legislation foreign to the substance of the bill itself. ·
It has been sometimes a common practice in
legislative bodies to attach to the regular appropriation bills for the service of the year, which
must be passed under penalty of embarrassing
the civil or military or naval service, riders embracing new legislation having no connection
with the appropriations. The objects of this
questionable practice are, first: to carry through

some measure which could not otherwise be reached during the session under the rules; secondly, to accomplish the amendment or repeal of existing laws; or, thirdly, to force upon the other House, when opposed in political opinion, a measure obnoxious to it and certain to be rejected if embodied in a separate bill. In Congress, this foisting upon appropriation bills of legislation foreign to their purpose, was carried so far that both Houses have adopted rules that no provision in any appropriation bill shall be in order which changes existing law, except such as is germane and retrenches expenditure. Another rule, in the House, prohibits amendment of any bill or resolution by incorporating in it the substance of any other bill or resolution pending.

In the British Parliament, riders to bills are called "tacks;" and, as the House of Commons has the constitutional power to grant supplies without interference by the Lords, they have sometimes abused this power by tacking to bills of supply enactments distasteful to the other House. These being contained in a bill which the House of Lords has no right to amend, place that body in the embarrassing position of suffering them to pass, or of obstructing the public service by the failure of its money supplies. This procedure has been resisted (and successfully) by protest, by conference and by the rejection of the bill. There have been no recent instances in which riders have been irregularly tacked to bills of supply in order to extort the consent of the Lords.

Seats.

This term, as used in an official sense, implies, first : the function of a Representative—as, to be admitted to his seat; to contest the seat of a member, etc.; secondly, in a literal sense, it is the chair, desk or bench occupied by a member. In Congress, the seats of Senators and Representatives are arm-chairs, each provided with a writing-desk. At the organization of each new Congress the seats are drawn by lot, those first drawn, of course, securing the choice of the most eligible seats. This is in the House of Representatives; in the Senate, there is no lot, but seats are "spoken for" or selected in advance, as vacancies occur, by individual Senators. In both branches of Congress, it is an established practice for members of the same party to sit near together, the Democrats occupying the seats to the right of the Chair, and the Republicans those on the left. In case, however, of a preponderant majority of one party being elected, the over-plus take seats among the ranks of their opponents.

In the British Parliament, and in the French Chambers, no desks are tolerated, and benches are used as seats. Public business receives undivided attention, and debate, in the true sense of the word, commands the ear of the assembly.

Substitute.

A motion to amend the main question by the adoption of a substitute is sometimes in order when nothing else in the nature of an amendment could be entertained. The rule of all parliamentary bodies is, not to admit an amendment in the third degree, *i. e.*, the right to offer amendments is exhausted when an amendment to the main question and an amendment to that amendment, have been brought before the assembly. A rule of the

House of Representatives, however, permits a substitute to be offered for an amendment in the second degree. This amendment, by way of substitute (to which one amendment may also be offered), cannot be voted on until the original matter is perfected. It may, however, be withdrawn at any time before the question is taken.

A substitute for any bill referred to a committee may be reported back from the committee with the original bill, in which case the substitute alone is to be considered by the House, and is treated as an original bill.

Table.

The motion to lay on the table is among the most frequently offered motions in public assemblies. It is not amendable nor debatable, and has precedence of all other motions, except one of privilege or of adjournment. The Chair must put the question at once, and, if carried, the matter is postponed until the assembly vote to take it from the table, which latter motion possesses no privilege. No surer method of defeating a measure when near the

end of the session of a deliberative body can
be found than to move that the question lie on
the table. In its primary sense, however, and
in practical usage in some assemblies, motions
to lay any matter on the table may be carried
without prejudice as to its merits, having the
effect simply to postpone it until a majority
are found ready to consider it.

In Congress, all business coming from the
other House, and communications from officers
of the government, are laid.on the table, unless
referred to a committee, or (in rare cases) considered without delay. A motion to lay any
bill or resolution on the table is in order on its
second or third reading. When a motion to
reconsider a previous vote is laid on the table,
the latter vote cannot be reconsidered, and is
held to be a final disposition of the matter.

The business on the Speaker's table embra-
ces : first, messages from the President, and other
executive communications ; second, messages
from the Senate, and amendments proposed by
the Senate to bills of the House ; third, bills
and resolutions from the Senate ; fourth, engrossed bills (which have passed the House),

and bills from the Senate on their third reading; fifth, bills and resolutions of the House. The Clerk of the House must make a weekly printed statement of the resolutions and bills upon the Speaker's table, with a note of the orders and proceedings of the House upon each.

Near the end of every session, there is a great accumulation of bills, resolutions, etc., both of the House and Senate, upon the Speaker's table, in every stage of progress toward enactment. The greater part of these must usually remain undisposed of, going to swell the great limbo of bills that do not become laws. By the Senate rule, there must lie on the table one day for consideration, all resolutions, reports of committees, and discharges of committees from the consideration of subjects, unless, by unanimous consent, the Senate shall otherwise direct.

Vetoes.

A bill, if retained by the President over ten days (unless Congress adjourns in the meantime), becomes a law upon a note of the fact registered with the bill in the Department of

State. If a bill is returned with the President's objections (which must be done within ten days after he receives it) it must be sent to the House in which it originated. The vote must again be taken on the vetoed bill in both Houses, and a majority of two-thirds of the members present and voting is required to make it a law. This was so decided in the 33d Congress, in 1856, in contravention to the claim that the constitutional majority of two-thirds implies two-thirds of the whole number of members.

A "pocket veto," so-called, implies the withholding of the signature of the President from a bill reaching him at about the close of a session, and which he chooses not to approve, Congress having in the meanwhile adjourned.

In Great Britain, while the Crown has the power, under the Constitution, to veto any act of Parliament, this prerogative has not been exercised since the year 1707.

Withdrawal.

The mover of any bill, resolution, motion or amendment, has the right to withdraw it if no one objects. If objected to, he may make a motion that he be granted permission to withdraw the matter submitted. If this motion is carried, the effect is to remove from consideration the matter and all subsidiary questions involved in it. The mover may also modify his motion before it is stated fully by the Chair, but not afterward, except on leave granted by the Assembly. By the rules of the House, any member may withdraw a motion or a bill at any time before the question is decided or amended, except after the previous question has been seconded. All incidental questions fall with the withdrawal of the main question.

Writs.

In Congress, a writ is a process of the House, signed by the Speaker, attested by the Clerk under the seal of the House, and served by the Sergeant-at-Arms. In the British Parliament, the writs for an election of new members are issued by the Speaker's warrant, addressed to the Clerk of the Crown, and by him forwarded to the local officers. Writs of summons for a new Parliament, after a dissolution of that body, are formally issued by the Crown under the actual authority of the Privy Council. Writs of summons must be issued at least thirty-five days before the day fixed by them for the assembling of the new Parliament.

CHAPTER IX

Debate.

THE proper control and limitation of debate is one of the functions of an assembly, to be always discreetly exercised through the presiding officer and the rules. A too rigorous confinement or suppression of debate is apt to be regarded with jealousy, not only as impairing individual liberty, but as checking that freedom of discussion essential to bring out all sides of a question, and conduce to its proper understanding by the assembly. How to avoid prolix, rambling and time-consuming speeches on the one hand, and at the same time give ample opportunity to discuss the merits of the question on the other, is the problem which continually calls for the tact of the presiding officer, and the judgment of the assembly. On this matter no stereotyped rule can be laid down, although, in societies and permanent bodies, it is usual to have some fixed limitation of the time allotted, both to written papers and to oral remarks.

These limitations may be laid down in the by-
laws of the association, or they may be adopted
from time to time at the meetings. It is to be
remarked, however, that whether the limits assigned to speeches or to papers be more or less
formal and permanent as rules, there is always
in practice a certain elasticity in applying them.
The watch of the presiding officer may keep
never so good time, but the tolerance or the
good nature of the Chair will sometimes restrain
him too long from the perhaps unwelcome announcement that a gentleman's time has expired.
Yet an undue indulgence to one speaker is unjust to others, and, where rules exist, it is the
right of every member to insist, if need be, upon
their enforcement by the presiding officer. It
is always possible, however, to secure to an assembly the pleasure of hearing all of a speech
or paper of unusual ability, or which provokes
uncommon interest, by some one moving that
the time of the speaker be extended. This can
be effected only by unanimous consent, one objection defeating the motion, which should be
put thus: "It is moved and seconded that the
time of the gentleman be extended. Is there

objection? The Chair hears none, and the gentleman will proceed." Or, if not agreed to unanimously, the Chair will announce: "Objection is made," when the speaker must take his seat, and the Chair will call for the next matter in order.

It is an invariable rule for speakers in debate, that all remarks must be addressed to the Chair, and not to the assembly. Speeches are to be confined to the question pending before the body; if rambling remarks are made, or other questions are introduced, any member may call the speaker to order, or the Chairman may interpose with the suggestion that debate is to be confined to the question before the assembly. Calling members by name is to be avoided; reference to others can easily be made with sufficient clearness, as, "*the gentleman who spoke last;*" "*the gentleman on my right;*" "*the gentleman who opened*," etc., although there is no rigid parliamentary rule to prevent using the actual names in ordinary assemblies. All personalities or severe reflections upon members which may be construed into personal attack, or reflections upon motives, are to be avoided. A disposition to quarrel being unfortunately found in the constitutions of some persons, one of whom may chance to be a member of a society or assembly where debate is customary, things are often said in the heat of discussion which provoke bitter animosities, and, perhaps, involve other members in an unseemly controversy. This is never productive of anything but harm to the objects of the association, and of regret to its members. How far a presiding officer can interpose to check personalities is a matter upon which no rule can be laid down, but it calls for the best discretion of the Chair. The only effectual safeguard against the consumption of time in fruitless wrangles, whether upon personalities, points of order, or methods of proceeding, is to be found in the good judgment and forbearance of the members, and their zealous adherence to the objects for which they come together.

The number of speeches which any one member can make on the same question is usually limited by regulation. This rests upon the obvious fact that an unlimited liberty of speech by any one member may prevent others from enjoying their just right to be heard. The more prevalent rule is to allow two speeches only to each member, although one only is sometimes the limitation. As to time, the limitation to ten minutes is more general than any other, although five-minute speeches, when in Committee of the Whole, have the sanction of the rules both of the Senate and of the House of Representatives. Permission to speak longer or more frequently may be granted by a majority of the assembly, if desired (or by unanimous consent), but the motion to grant this permission is not debatable. A very proper proceeding is for the assembly to fix in advance an hour at which debate shall be closed, thus securing a most desirable dispatch of business.

The motions which are not debatable are the following :

1. The motion for the previous question.

2. To lay on the table, or to take from the table any matter.

3. To suspend a rule, or the rules.

4. An appeal from the decision of the

Chair, when it relates to violation of the rules, or to disorder, or to the priority of business, or when the previous question was pending at the time the appeal was taken.

5. To adjourn.

6. To fix the time to which to adjourn (whenever another question is before the assembly).

7. To take a recess.

8. Questions of order arising after a motion is made for the previous question, or upon undebatable questions.

9. Questions relating to the priority of business.

It is a well recognized rule of courtesy that the mover of any proposition is first entitled to the floor to discuss it. That the mover is again entitled to the floor to close the debate, though less generally recognized, is made a rule of the House of Representatives, in the case of the member reporting the measure under consideration from a committee. The same rule entitles him to one hour to close, notwithstanding he may have used an hour in opening.

After the question has been opened by the

proposer, the presiding officer of the assembly is to recognize other speakers successively; and, although there is no fixed rule of parliamentary law prescribing it, it is recognized as proper, in case of two or more rising at once to speak, for the presiding officer to recognize the member farthest from the Chair. It is also usual, though not fixed by rule, for those favoring and opposing the proposition before the assembly to alternate in speaking.

The House of Representatives has what is known as the one-hour rule, first adopted in 1847, which provides that no member can occupy more than one hour in debate on any question in the House. It would be a great mistake to infer that this secures any member who wishes to be heard the right to occupy an hour. The life of a Congress is short, and in practice a very few members only secure an hour, the rest being cut off by the previous question, usually asking and procuring "leave to print," or being allowed a few minutes of the time of the member who is entitled to an hour to close the debate. Another rule of the House is that no member shall speak more than once to the question, unless he be the mover, in which case he may speak in reply, but not until every member choosing shall have spoken. Both of these last named rules, however, may be and often are suspended by unanimous consent (unless the House is pressing toward a vote). Another rule provides that the Speaker is to name the member who is first to speak, as " *the gentleman from Maine,*" etc., when two or more members claim the floor at once. No debate is allowed after the House has ordered the previous question, except one speech from the member reporting the measure; but, as he is entitled to an entire hour, he frequently yields a certain number of minutes of his time to several members for short speeches. No member may call another by name in debate, or call attention to the views of the other House (¹), but both of these rules are transgressed with great frequency. Both Houses have a rule that any member transgressing in debate the rules of the body, shall be

(1) Jefferson's Manual says: " It is a breach of order in debate to notice what has been said on the same subject in the other House, or the particular votes or majority on it there ; because the opinion of each House should be left to its own independency, not to be influenced by the proceedings of the other."

called to order by the presiding officer (or any member may call him to order), when he must sit down, and cannot proceed unless leave is granted. This leave must be on motion, and determined without debate. The words excepted to must be indicated by the member calling to order, and taken down in writing and read at the Clerk's desk. In the Senate, no Senator may interrupt another in debate without his 'consent, and to obtain such consent he must first address the presiding officer. Rule 14, of the House of Representatives, requires that "a member shall confine himself to the question under debate, and avoid personality," but in Committee of the Whole on the state of the Union, he is not bound to confine himself to the question under debate, except when a special order is pending.

In the Senate, debate is without limit unless a special order is made curtailing the length of speeches, and when considering the calendar of bills and resolutions as a daily order, when each Senator is entitled to speak but five minutes, and only once upon any question. No Senator can speak more than twice on any question on the same day, without leave of the Senate. Another Senate rule provides that during the morning hour motions to proceed to consider any matter must be decided without debate upon the merits of the subject proposed to be taken up.

Interruptions in the House to the member speaking are quite frequent, but do not appear to be provided for in the rules. The customary mode of interruption is for a member to call out: "Will the gentleman yield?" or "Mr. Speaker, will the gentleman from ——yield to me for a question?" If the member holding the floor refuses, the Chair announces: "The gentleman from —— declines to yield," and the speech is proceeded with.

A rule of the House permits members to speak, when debating, at their seats, or from any part of the floor, or at the Clerk's desk.

In the British Parliament, while the Speaker must be addressed in the Commons, a peer addresses the House of Lords in general—as, "*My Lords.*" Debate in the Lords depends upon the will of the body, which may give preference to any peer seeking the floor. In the House of

Commons, the Speaker must recognize the member who first rises. As it often happens that several members rise at once, the member who is first in his eye is called upon. The rule of the Commons is that only one speech from any member on the same question can be heard except in Committee of the Whole. No member is permitted to be called by name in either House ; the Lords are referred to by their rank, as " *the noble Earl;*" members are designated in the other House by the place they represent, as " *the honorable gentleman, the member for Manchester.*" While speaking, members of the Lords and Commons remove their hats, and resume them upon concluding and taking their seats. No reading of written speeches is permitted in either House of Parliament. Extracts from documents may be read, but members must debate questions in the literal sense without reading manuscript remarks.

This rule is almost reversed in Congress, where written speeches are practically rather the rule in both Houses, and debate in its legitimate sense the exception.

In France, members of the *Corps Législatif*

(6)

speak from the tribune, not from their seats. A list of the Deputies proposing to speak at any session is kept by the President, who recognizes them in the order of their inscription on the list, except that members are to speak alternately for and against the measure under consideration. This rule does not prevail in the parliamentary bodies either of England or America. The Ministers are awarded the floor whenever they claim it, although it may interfere with the sequence of the list of speakers; but a member of the opposition may always follow the speech of a Minister. The rules prohibit disorder or clamor during discussion, but the rule is largely violated. If the Chamber becomes tumultuous, and the efforts of the President to restore order are ineffective, he puts on his hat; if the disorder continues, he declares the session adjourned for an hour, at the end of which members resume their places. If the tumult breaks out again, the President must adjourn the Chamber to the next day.

CHAPTER X

Voting.

THE sense of an assembly is always to be ascertained by its votes. In general, whether at formal or informal meetings, the presiding officer is to put every question to vote either without debate (if the rules so require), or, if it is a debatable question, when members have ceased to speak, or when the time allotted for debate is exhausted. In calling for a vote, it is usual for the Chair to inquire : " Are you ready for the question ? " Which is usually responded to by one or more members calling out : " Question ! " The following are the principal forms of taking a vote :

1. *Viva voce*, when the presiding officer calls successively the ayes and the noes, and declares the motion carried or lost, according to the preponderance of voices.

2. (In a small assembly), by a show of hands, each side in succession holding up the right hand and being counted.

3. By calling for the ayes to rise and stand until counted, after which the ayes are required to be seated, and those in the negative to rise for a count by the Chair.

4. By tellers, the Chair appointing two members to count the voters as they pass between them, those in favor of the measure going first, and those opposed after, the number on each side being reported by the tellers and announced by the Chair.

5. By calling the yeas and nays, each member answering *aye* or *no*, in alphabetical order, when the vote is registered in a formal record, summed up by the Clerk or Secretary, and announced by the Chair.

6. By ballot, or secret written vote, the folded papers being collected by the Secretary or by members appointed for the purpose. The last named form of voting is used in balloting for members, or in the election of officers or committees by the assembly itself.

When the assembly has not ordered the vote to be taken in any particular way, it is customary for the Chair to call for it *viva voce*. If in doubt as to which side is in the majority, or if any member calls for a division, the Chair next asks the members to vote *aye* or *no* by rising. Taking the vote by passing through tellers is peculiar to legislative bodies. Whenever a record of the vote is desired, any member may call for the yeas and nays ; and taking a vote in this manner is a constitutional right or obligation in both Houses of Congress, when required by one-fifth of the members present. In ordinary assemblies, however, it appears to require a majority to order a vote to be taken by yeas and nays.

Taking a vote or making a nomination " by acclamation," although common in political conventions, is hardly worthy of the dignity of a deliberative body. And the prevalent usage of moving to make a nomination unanimous has been severely criticised as suppressing the convictions of the minority who have been out-voted.

In general, a majority of the votes cast is sufficient for the adoption of any proposition. But rules are sometimes adopted by which the following motions require a vote of two-thirds of the assembly in order to carry them :

1. To amend or to suspend the rules.

2. To order the previous question, or to limit debate, (usually requires a majority only).

3. To consider any question out of its proper order as fixed by the order of business.

4. To appoint a special order in advance to consider any question.

5. To decline to consider a question.

6. To make certain nominations (¹).

The general principle is, that no motion having the effect to change the established rules and customs should be carried by a mere majority, but should have the sanction of approximate unanimity. As the right of free discussion upon the merits of any question before taking action thereon is an established custom, the limiting or closing of debate is sometimes held to require a two-thirds vote, although in the House of Representatives (and as a general

---

(1) In the National Conventions of the Democratic party, a majority consisting of two-thirds of the delegates has been required to nominate candidates for President and Vice-President, ever since 1832. The majority rule, however, has always prevailed in the Republican National Conventions. What is known as the unit rule in these Conventions, requiring the vote of each State delegation to be cast as a unit (*i. e.*, all for some one candidate dictated by the majority of the delegation), has been practically abandoned for the freer system of permitting each delegate to vote as he pleases.

rule elsewhere), the previous question is ordered by a simple majority. In the Senate, where there is no previous question, not even a two-thirds vote could abridge the privilege of debate.

A two-thirds vote of Senators present is required to convict on an impeachment, to expel a member, to ratify treaties, to pass a bill over the veto, and to propose amendments to the Constitution. The same is required in the House in cases of expulsion, veto, constitutional amendments, making a special order suspending the rules, to dispense with call of committees in the morning hour, and to dispense with private business on Fridays. Every Senator is required to vote when the yeas and nays are called; if he declines, he is required to assign his reasons therefor, after which the presiding officer submits the question to the Senate : " Shall the Senator, for the reasons assigned by him, be excused from voting? " which must be decided without debate. No Senator is permitted to vote after the result is announced by the President, and he cannot give reasons for his vote; these two rules cannot be suspended even by unanimous consent. A Senator "may, for sufficient reasons, with unanimous consent, change or withdraw his vote."

In the House, votes on minor questions are almost always taken in the first instance *viva voce*, by the sound. If this is inconclusive, the Speaker calls for a rising vote, either of his own motion, or at the call of any member for a division. After this, when the vote is announced, any member dissatisfied with the result may demand tellers, the rule providing that a vote must be taken by tellers if demanded by one-fifth of a quorum. It is customary when, on a division, less than half the House are counted as voting, for the Speaker at once to order tellers. He must name two members on opposite sides of the question to act as tellers; these two meet and shake hands in the middle aisle; the Chair requests all members voting in the affirmative to pass between the tellers, who count them and report to the Clerk's desk; next, the negative voters are summoned to pass between the tellers; this count being reported, the Chair declares the result. No record of individual names is kept in voting by tellers, or by rising.

In the Senate, no vote is ever taken by tellers.

In the House of Commons, the Speaker appoints two tellers from each party (four in all) to count the members when dividing the House, when the *viva voce* vote is not accepted. Members in favor of the measure before the House, then withdraw to the lobby on the right, and those opposed withdraw to the left. As members file back into the House, they are counted by the tellers and their names recorded by the Clerks. The result is announced by the Speaker, and alphabetical lists of the names are printed with the votes and proceedings. This system combines the yea and nay vote with a vote by tellers. No member is allowed to vote who was not in the House when the question was put; but a " division bell " is rung by the doorkeeper whenever the House is about to divide. This signal is heard through the neighboring rooms, and scattered members hasten to be present at the division before the doors are locked. The time allowed for this notice is two minutes, measured by a sand-glass; when that has run out, the doors are at once closed, and the Speaker must again put the question before

the House by ayes and noes, as the rule provides that no absentees on the first call can vote
unless the question is again put. If the numbers on a division are equal, the Speaker of the
Commons must give the casting vote. In the
House of Lords, if there is a tie, the question.
is lost.

In the French Chambers, any member may
require a division, which, in the first instance,
is always by a rising vote. This vote is in
order upon all questions, unless twenty members demand an open ballot, or fifty members a
secret ballot; or, unless the vote by rising, after
being taken twice, results in a tie, in which
case any member may demand a ballot. In
the open ballot, each member is furnished with
white tickets for affirmative votes, and blue
tickets for negative, on all of which his name
is printed. The messengers collect these ballots in an urn, which is opened at the tribune,
the Secretaries counting the ballots of each
color, and the President announcing the result,
while the names printed on the tickets furnish
a record of each member's vote. The secret
ballot is taken by white and black balls—the

white signifying votes in the affirmative, and the black the negative. Members deposit their balls in an urn, when the Secretaries turn them out into a basket, and count the black and white balls, announcing the result to the President, who proclaims it to the Chamber.

In Congress, it is a constitutional requirement that the yeas and nays shall be entered on the journal in both Houses when the vote is taken on any bill vetoed by the President; also, that the yeas and nays in either House shall be entered on the journals when desired by one-fifth of the members present. In the House, it is usual for members to demand a vote by yeas and nays on all important questions, or when it is sought to make a record, or when not satisfied with the result of a division by other methods, or, finally and very frequently, when members in the opposition wish to consume time, or to delay the passage of a measure. The rules of the House imperatively require that the vote shall be taken by yeas and nays on the passage of general appropriation bills, revenue bills, and bills for the improvement of rivers and harbors. Usage permits the yeas and nays to be demanded even while a vote is being taken on a division by tellers, or after the announcement, before passing to any other business. It is not in order to repeat a demand for the yeas and nays which has been once refused. No debate or remark or point of order can interrupt the roll-call, after the first member has answered to his name, on a call for the yeas and nays. A member may change his vote at any time before the Chair has finally announced the decision of the question; and he may demand that an erroneous record of his vote be corrected, after the announcement of the result, if the House has not proceeded to other business. Otherwise, the correction must be made on the journal when it is read for approval or amendment the next morning. The time consumed in a call of the yeas and nays is nearly forty minutes. It includes calling the roll by surnames (for the required record), checking the names as members answer Aye or No, summing up, calling of absentees a second time, announcement of members paired, and reading the names of all those voting in the affirmative and negative, by the Clerk. Various ingenious plans to curtail this enormous waste of time by the roll-call have been proposed, the most modern invention being an annunciator with electric wires, the member touching a button at his desk, and the vote being recorded instantaneously, yea or nay, for the whole House. The House, however, has never countenanced any substitute for *viva voce* voting, although the roll-calls so frequently repeated on party divisions sometimes consume more than half the working time of a day's session. After completion of the roll-call, the names of members who have failed to answer must be called again, when the announcement of " pairs " is in order.

The pairing of members in a legislative body is an agreement between two members of opposite politics, or who would vote on opposite sides of any question, to withhold their votes; such pairs leaving the result of the vote unaffected. One or both of the members thus paired may be absent. This system has never been recognized by parliamentary rules until the 46th Congress (in 1880), when the 8th rule of the House of Representatives required that pairs should be announced by the Clerks from a written list furnished him, signed by the member making the statement. Usually each party appoints a committee of one, whose duty it is to secure and record pairs for absent or indisposed members.

In Parliament, pairing prevails to a greater extent than in Congress, members pairing with each other not only upon particular measures, but in case of absenteeism, for weeks and even months at a time. The system has long prevailed, but it is not recognized by any rule of either House of Parliament, being merely a private arrangement. In the lower House of Congress, pairs between members are published in the official record on each division of yeas and nays. They are not recognized by the Senate rules, and are not entered in the journal with the votes, although long and constantly in use. But Senators frequently announce that they are paired, as a reason for not voting.

Every member of the House is required to vote, unless excused on a motion made before division and decided without debate, or unless he has direct personal or pecuniary interest in the event of the question.

When the vote in an assembly is evenly divided on any question, the general parliamentary rule is that the question is lost. This is always the case if the presiding officer has already voted as a member of the body; nor is it settled that a presiding officer who has not voted, has the casting vote in case of a tie, unless this power of decision is conferred upon him by the constitution or rules governing the body.

In the Senate, the Vice-President has no vote when presiding over the Senate, unless that body be equally divided, when he may cast his vote to decide the question. But this is a constitutional provision. The rules of the Senate confer no power on the President *pro tempore* to decide questions as presiding officer, and if the votes are equal, the question is lost. This goes upon the principle that the President *pro tempore* votes as a Senator, and in fact his name is always called when the yeas and nays are ordered. In the House of Representatives, the Speaker is required to vote only when his vote would be decisive if counted, or when the House votes by ballot ; and in all cases of a tie vote, the question is lost. Thus, if 120 votes are cast on each side of a pending question, and the Speaker holds with the affirmative, he must vote, thus carrying the question ; if he holds with the negative, however, his vote would not alter the result, the question being already lost, and he is not required to vote. The Speaker has the right to direct his name to be called on any question, if he desires to be recorded, but in practice his right to vote is seldom exercised, unless, in important questions, he desires to make a record.

If the question that there is no quorum present, be raised by any member when a vote is taken, the Senate rule provides that the Chair shall direct the roll to be called to ascertain the presence of a quorum. If it is found that a quorum is not present, no vote can be taken except by unanimous consent, until a quorum appears.

In the House, a majority of the members chosen constitutes a quorum, which thus consists of 163 members, the full number of the present House being 325. If the question of the presence of a quorum is not raised, the journal may be read, and motions, debate and other proceedings may go on until some call for a division or vote discloses the absence of a quorum. After that, no motion is in order except for a call of the House (to compel the attendance of a majority of the body), or to adjourn. By the 15th rule of the House, in the absence of a quorum, fifteen members, including the Speaker, are authorized to compel the attendance of absentees.

The quorum of a Committee of the Whole House is the same as that of the House; and if the committee finds itself without a quorum, the chairman must cause the roll to be called, when the committee must rise, and the chairman must report the names of the absentees to the House, to be entered on the journal. If, however, a quorum appears on a call of the roll, the committee must resume its sitting without further order of the House.

The quorum of the House on one extraordinary occasion is required by the Constitution (Article 12) to consist of a member or

members from two-thirds of the States. This
is in case of the election of a President devolv-
ing upon the House of Representatives, in consequence of no candidate receiving a majority
of the Electoral vote. In choosing the President, each State has one vote, and a majority
of all the States is necessary to a choice. In
like manner, the quorum of the Senate, for the
purpose of choosing the Vice-President, is made
by the Constitution to consist of two-thirds of
the whole number of Senators, a majority of
whom is necessary to a choice.

Voting in legislative bodies is rarely required
to be by ballot, and in this country balloting,
in the case of parliamentary bodies, appears
to be confined to the election of officers. In cor-
porate bodies, both private and municipal, election by ballot has long prevailed, while in deliberative and legislative bodies, where questions
are decided in the affirmative or negative, the
reason for the ballot is not apparent. Voting
should be open, not secret, in parliamentary
bodies, to enforce just responsibility, and to bring
the acts of their representatives before each
constituency in the clearest manner. In thir-

teen States, there is a constitutional provision requiring the Legislature to vote *viva voce*; these are Alabama, California, Florida, Georgia, Indiana, Kansas, Kentucky, Louisiana, Nevada, North Carolina, Pennsylvania, Tennessee and Texas. In the other States, the Legislature is left to regulate its own methods of voting.

The number of votes required to pass an act in a legislative body varies greatly. The constitutions of some States require, in order to render a law valid, that it shall have been passed by a majority of all the members elected to the Legislature. In both branches of Congress, however, a majority of all the members present (if a quorum of the whole House) may pass any measure which is in order under the rules. The result is, that a law may be actually made by little more than one-fourth of the Senators and Representatives elected. In fact, twenty Senators and eighty-two Representatives, voting in the affirmative, may pass the most important act of legislation, in strict conformity to the rules. The rule that a majority is required to elect a Senator, in State Legislatures, is prescribed by the laws of the United States.

In the British Parliament, there is no requirement as to the number of votes necessary to
render valid an act of Parliament. On the contrary, such rules as do prevail (although liable
to change) permit forty members in the House
of Commons to constitute a quorum for legislation, and three only in the House of Lords.

In France, an absolute majority of the whole
number of members elected to the Legislative
Body is required to render any act they may
pass valid.

APPENDIX.

Brief Example of a Meeting Conducted under Parliamentary Rules.

[Designed to illustrate oniy the simpler forms of proceeding, and the elementary rules for conducting business.]

A member. The time appointed for this meeting having arrived, gentlemen will please come to order. I move that Mr. A. B. take the Chair.

Another member. I second the motion.

First member. It is moved and seconded that Mr. A. B. act as Chairman; as many as are in favor of the motion will please say Aye.

(A general response is heard in the affirmative.)

First member. As many as are opposed to the motion will say No.

(Few or no voices in the negative.)

First member. The motion is carried, and Mr. A. B. will please take the Chair.

(Or, a member calling the meeting to order, may ask: " Will some one nominate a Chairman to preside over

189

this meeting?" Which being done, he puts the question to vote as before.)

Mr. A. B. (in the Chair, with or without a speech of thanks, or remarks upon the business upon which the assembly is convened) : Gentlemen will please come to order. Is it the pleasure of the meeting to elect a Secretary ?

A member. I nominate Mr. C. D. as Secretary.

Another member. I second the motion.

The Chair. It is moved and seconded that Mr. C. D. act as Secretary of this meeting. As many as are in favor of the motion will say Aye. (After a pause.) As many as are opposed to the motion will say No.

The ayes have it, and Mr. C. D. will please act as Secretary.

(If several names are proposed, either for Chairman or Secretary, the vote should be called for upon the names in succession, beginning with the first name proposed.)

The Secretary takes a seat near the Chair. He should have a table provided for notes, and a record book or journal, or blank paper, for the proceedings.

The Chair. Is it the pleasure of the meeting to appoint any committees ?

Mr. E. F. Mr. Chairman, I move that a committee of three be appointed on the order of business, and a committee of five on resolutions.

A member. I second that motion.

The Chair. Gentlemen, it is moved and seconded that a committee of three be appointed on the order of business, and a committee of five to prepare resolutions for the consideration of the meeting. Are you ready for the question?

(Amid calls of Question! Question!)

A member. Mr. Chairman, I move to amend the first motion by striking out " three " and inserting " five," so that the committee on business may embrace five members.

Another member. I second the amendment.

The Chair. It is moved to amend the resolution by striking out "three" and inserting "five." As many as are in favor of the amendment will say Aye. (After a pause.) Those opposed to the amendment will say No. (After a pause.) The ayes have it, and the amendment is adopted. The question now recurs on the original motion as amended, that a committee of five members be appointed on the order of business, and one of five members on resolutions. As many as are in favor of the adoption of the motion will say Aye. (A general *aye.*) As many as are opposed will say No. The ayes have it, and the motion is adopted. How shall these committees be appointed?

Several members. By the Chair.

The Chairman. It is moved that the Chair appoint the members of these two committees. All in favor of that motion will say Aye; contrary, No. The ayes have it, and the motion is carried. The Chair appoints as the committee on order of business, Messrs. E. F. chairman (and four others, naming them), and as a committee on resolutions, the Chair appoints Messrs. G. H.

chairman (and four others, naming them). The committees are requested to confer and report to the meeting as early as convenient. (The members appointed on each committee, headed by its chairman, withdraw for consultation.)

A member. Mr. Chairman, I move the adoption of the following resolution (reading it).

The Chair. The resolution will be referred to the committee on resolutions when appointed. (It is placed in the hands of the Secretary.)

A member. Gentlemen, on this important and interesting occasion——

The Chairman. The gentleman is out of order; he will please address the Chair.

The member. Mr. Chairman, on this occasion so important to——

The Chairman. The gentleman is again out of order; there is no motion before the meeting.

Another member. Mr. Chairman, I move that the gentleman be invited to address the meeting.

The Chairman. The motion is made that Mr. —— be invited to speak. Is there objection? (After a pause.) The Chair hears none; (and Mr. —— makes a speech followed, perhaps, by other gentlemen, who speak by unanimous consent).

(During the speaking, there being much confusion in the hall)—

A member. Mr. Chairman, I rise to a point of order.

The Chair. The gentleman will state his point of order.

The member. My point of order is, that we, in this part of the hall, can hear very little of what is going on on account of the talking and moving about.

The Chair (rapping on the table). The point of order is well taken. The meeting will be in order. Members will take their seats and suspend conversation. (After a pause, quiet being restored)—

The Chair. The gentleman will now proceed.

(Here the speaking is interrupted by the return of the committee on the order of business, headed by its chairman, who addresses the Chair):

Mr. Chairman, the committee on the order of business have agreed upon a report (handing up a paper).

The Chair. The Secretary will read the report of the committee.

The Secretary reads :

1. The officers already chosen are continued as permanent Chairman and Secretary of the meeting.

2. No member may speak more than once to the same question.

3. Debate is limited to ten minutes for each speech.

4. When the previous question is ordered by a majority vote, debate shall at once cease, and the Chair shall take the vote on the pending question.

5. In ruling upon points of order or precedence, the Chair is to be governed by the rules of the House of Representatives, when applicable.

The Chair. You have heard the report of the committee. What is the pleasure of the meeting ?

A member. Mr. Chairman, I move that the report be adopted.

Another member. I second that motion.

The Chair. It is moved and seconded that the report just read on the order of business be adopted as the rules for the conduct of business. Are you ready for the question?

Several members. Question! Question!

The Chair. As many as are in favor of the adoption of the report will say Aye.

(Loud responses of *aye.*)

As many as are opposed to the adoption of the report will say No.

(No response).

The Chair. The ayes have it, and the report of the committee on the order of business is adopted.

(The committee on resolutions, through their chairman, report a series of five resolutions, embodying the sense of the meeting on the subject before it.)

The Chair. The Secretary (or the chairman of the committee), will read the resolutions.

The Chair (after the reading). The resolutions are before the meeting. Are there any remarks to be made upon them?

(After discussion, and the adoption or rejection of several amendments)—

The Chair. If there are no further remarks or motions, the Chair will put the question on the adoption of the resolutions.

A member. Mr. Chairman, I move a division of the question. I call for a separate vote on the second resolution.

The Chair. A separate vote is called for on the second resolution. As many as are in favor of taking the question separately on that resolution will say Aye. (After a pause.) Those of a contrary opinion will say No. The ayes have it. As many as are in favor of the adoption of the second resolution will say Aye. (Responses of *aye*.) As many as are opposed to the adoption of the second resolution will say No. The ayes appear to have it.

(Calls of Division! Division!)

The Chair. As many as are in favor of the adoption of the second resolution will rise and stand until they are counted.

The Chair. Thirty-one gentlemen in the affirmative. The ayes will be seated and the noes will rise. (After a count.)

The Chair. There are fifty-two voting in the negative. The resolution is lost. The question now recurs on the adoption of the other resolutions as amended, leaving out the second resolution. As many as are in favor of the adoption of the resolutions will say Aye. (A general response of *aye*.) As many as are opposed to the adoption of the resolutions will say No. (A few scattering noes are heard.)

The Chair. The ayes have it, and the resolutions are adopted.

A member. Mr. Chairman, I now move that the meeting proceed to consider (stating some question).

Another member. I second the motion.

The Chair. It is moved and seconded that the meeting consider (the subject named).

A third member. Mr. Chairman, I move that the subject referred to in the motion be indefinitely postponed.

The Chair. The question is on the motion to postpone indefinitely the consideration of ——; (puts the question in form as before, and declares it carried or lost, as the case may be).

A member. Mr. Chairman, I move the adoption of the following resolution (reading it).

Another member. I second the motion.

The Chair. It is moved and seconded that the resolution sent to the Chair be adopted; are you ready for the question?

(A member rises to debate the resolution, and is replied to. After considerable discussion, developing much difference of opinion)—

A member. Mr. Chairman, I move to lay the resolution on the table.

Another member. I second the motion.

The Chair. It is moved and seconded that the resolution before the meeting be laid on the table.

A member. Mr. Chairman, I rise to oppose the motion to lay on the table, which would have the effect—

The Chair. The gentleman is not in order; a motion to lay on the table is not debatable.

A member. Mr. Chairman, I rise to a point of order.

The Chair. The gentleman will state the point of order.

The member. I make the point of order that discussion should be allowed on the motion, that the meeting may know the reasons why they are asked not to consider it.

The Chair. The Chair overrules the point of order. No discussion is in order upon a motion to lay on the table.

The member. I appeal from the decision of the Chair.

The Chair. The Chair will put the question on the appeal, only remarking that his decision in overruling the point of order and holding that the motion to lay on the table is not debatable, is based upon the rule of the House of Representatives, sustained by the uniform usage of parliamentary bodies. The question is: "Shall the decision of the Chair stand as the judgment of the meeting?" All who are in favor of sustaining the Chair will say Aye. (General response of *aye*.) Those opposed to the ruling of the Chair will say No. (One negative vote.)

The Chair. The ayes have it, and the decision of the Chair is sustained. The question now recurs upon the motion to lay upon the table the resolution sent to the Chair. As many as are in favor of laying the resolution on the table will say Aye. (After a pause.) As many as are opposed to laying the resolution on the table will say No. The ayes have it, and the resolution is laid on the table.

A member. Mr. Chairman, I hold in my hand a paper which I ask permission, at this stage of the proceedings, to read.

The Chair. That requires unanimous consent, or, in its absence, leave to read by a vote of the assembly. Is there objection?

A member. I object.

The Chair. Objection is made.

A member. Mr. Chairman, I move that leave be granted to read the paper in question. (The motion is seconded.)

The Chair. It is moved and seconded that permission be granted to read the paper offered.

The member who made the motion. Mr. Chairman, I rise to withdraw the motion that the paper be read.

The Chair. The Chair thinks that the motion cannot be withdrawn if objection is made, except by leave to withdraw, after putting the question of such leave to vote. Is there objection to the withdrawal of the motion?

A member. I object.

Another member. Mr. Chairman, I think, with all due respect to the ruling of the Chair, that in this case he is mistaken. We have adopted the rules of the House of Representatives, wherever applicable. Rule XVI of the House Manual prescribes that "when a motion has been made *   *   * it shall then be in possession of the House, but may be withdrawn at any time before a decision or amendment."

The Chair. The Chair stands corrected. The rule is as stated by the gentleman, and, of course, overrides the more generally received practice that the mover of any question cannot withdraw it after it has been stated by the Chair and is in possession of the assembly. The motion is withdrawn, and there is no question before the meeting.

A member. Mr. Chairman, I move that we do now adjourn.

Another member. Mr. Chairman, before that motion is put I desire—

The Chair. The gentleman is out of order; the motion to adjourn is not debatable, but must be put without delay. The only way in which other business or debate can be brought forward is by voting down the motion for adjournment. As many as are in favor of the motion to adjourn will say Aye. (Loud responses of *aye.*) As many as are opposed to the motion to adjourn will say No. (A feeble response.) The ayes have it, and the meeting stands adjourned.

INDEX.

201